COMPANION PLANTING FOR BEGINNERS

Creating Eco-Friendly Gardens for Sustainable, Healthier Plants: Foster Biodiversity and Minimize Chemicals - Tackle Pest Problems Naturally

TERRA VERDE WRITERS

Contents

Introduction ... 7

1. THE FOUNDATIONS OF COMPANION PLANTING ... 11
1.1 The Philosophy Behind Companion Planting ... 12
1.2 Decoding the Science: How Plants Benefit Each Other ... 14
1.3 Companion Planting Myths vs. Facts ... 16
1.4 Creating Your First Companion Plant Pairing ... 19
1.5 The Role of Pollinators in Companion Planting ... 21
1.6 Understanding Companion Planting Zones ... 23

2. PLANNING YOUR COMPANION GARDEN ... 27
2.1 Assessing Your Space ... 27
2.2 Designing Your Companion Planting Layout ... 30
2.3 Companion Plants for Small Spaces and Balconies ... 32
2.4 Seasonal Planning for Year-Round Harvests ... 35
2.5 Water Management in Companion Planting ... 37
2.6 Sunlight and Shade: Maximizing Photosynthesis ... 40

3. PLANT PAIRINGS AND THEIR BENEFITS ... 43
3.1 The Best Companion Plants for Tomatoes ... 43
3.2 Nurturing Your Soil: Nitrogen-Fixing Plant Partners ... 47
3.3 Pest Repelling Plant Pairings That Work ... 49
3.4 Companion Flowers: More Than Just Pretty Faces ... 51
3.5 Maximizing Small Spaces with Strategic Pairings ... 53
3.6 Unusual and Exotic Companion Plant Pairings ... 55

4. IMPLEMENTING COMPANION PLANTING IN YOUR GARDEN ... 59
4.1 Preparing the Soil for Companion Planting ... 59
4.2 Seed Starting and Transplanting Tips ... 62
4.3 Natural Solutions to Common Pest Problems ... 65

    4.4 Watering Techniques for Companion Planted Gardens   68
    4.5 Mulching: Types and Techniques for Companion Planting   71
    4.6 Seasonal Care and Maintenance of Companion Plants   73

5. ADVANCED COMPANION PLANTING STRATEGIES   79
    5.1 Creating a Permaculture Garden with Companion Planting   79
    5.2 Bio-Intensive Companion Planting Methods   82
    5.3 Companion Planting for Greenhouse Gardens   85
    5.4 Utilizing Vertical Space in Companion Planting   88
    5.5 Companion Planting and Hydroponic Systems   91
    5.6 Succession Planting and Crop Rotation Strategies   93

6. TACKLING COMMON GARDENING CHALLENGES   97
    6.1 Dealing with Shade: Companion Plants That Thrive Together   97
    6.2 Soil Health: Companion Plants for Soil Rejuvenation   99
    6.3 Managing Overcrowding in Compact Spaces   102
    6.4 Companion Planting to Attract Beneficial Insects   104
    6.5 Drought-Tolerant Companion Planting   106
    6.6 Cold-Climate Companion Planting Strategies   108

7. COMPANION PLANTING FOR SPECIFIC GOALS   111
    7.1 Companion Planting for Maximum Yield   111
    7.2 Building a Pollinator-Friendly Garden   114
    7.3 Companion Plants for Natural Pest Control   117
    7.4 Companion Planting for Herbal Gardens   118
    7.5 Edible Flowers and Companion Planting   121
    7.6 Companion Planting for Medicinal Plants   123

8. THE FUTURE OF COMPANION PLANTING   127
    8.1 Innovations in Companion Planting   127
    8.2 Community and Social Aspects of Companion Planting   129
    8.3 Companion Planting as a Family Activity   132

8.4 The Environmental Impact of Companion Planting	134
8.5 Companion Planting and Wildlife Conservation	137
8.6 Continuing Your Companion Planting Journey	139
Conclusion	143
References	145

Introduction

Step into a garden where every leaf and bloom has a role in a grander scheme, where the air is alive with the buzz of life, and the earth itself seems to sing with vitality. This isn't just any garden; it's a carefully orchestrated symphony of plants that thrive together, warding off pests and sharing nutrients in a stunning display of nature's resilience and wisdom. Welcome to companion planting, a practice where diversity leads to beauty and a robust ecosystem.

I'm someone who has journeyed from the initial curiosity of planting a few seeds to becoming a fervent advocate for sustainable gardening. Through years of digging, planting, and nurturing, I've learned that gardening can be as stimulating to the gardener as it is to the earth. It's my passion to share this knowledge, especially with you, who may be standing where I once did—eager to start but unsure how. I understand this journey's challenges and joys and am here to guide you through it.

This book is crafted to be your guide, aiming to simplify the rich complexities of companion planting. Whether you have a sprawling yard or a modest balcony, I'm here to show you how to harness the natural benefits of planting together. Companion planting offers a plethora of advantages—it enhances biodiversity, reduces the need for chemical interventions, and naturally manages pests. For instance, planting garlic near roses saves the roses from aphids and benefits the garlic, making it a practical and chemical-free solution to common gardening woes.

I understand that beginning this journey might seem daunting. You might need help choosing the right plants or make mistakes—it's natural. This book addresses these fears by breaking down the process into manageable, straightforward steps. Each chapter builds on the last, from selecting your plants to understanding their needs and behaviours in the garden.

What sets this book apart is its approachability and practicality. I've distilled scientific research and personal experiences into straightforward, actionable advice. You'll find visual aids to help illustrate concepts and real-life examples that demonstrate the principles of companion planting from my own trials and successes. This book is not just about theory; it's about practical, hands-on gardening that you can start implementing today.

You're not just starting a gardening project as you turn these pages. You're initiating a profound transformation in your gardening approach and relationship with the natural world. This book is not just a method but a catalyst for this inspiring change.

I encourage you to dive in with enthusiasm and an open heart. Let curiosity be your guide as you explore your garden's synergistic potential. The path may be lined with trials, but the rewards—lush, vibrant plant life and a deeper bond with nature—are worth the journey.

To inspire and propel you forward, remember these words from the poet Rumi:

Let the beauty of what you love be what you do.

There's much to love in the dance of companion planting and much to do. Let's begin this beautiful journey together.

ONE

The Foundations of Companion Planting

Have you ever wondered how plants, like people, can benefit immensely from good company? Just as we thrive in a supportive community, plants can grow better and stronger when paired thoughtfully with suitable companions. This fundamental idea is not just a modern gardening trend but is deeply rooted in ancient wisdom and practices, connecting us to a rich tradition that spans generations. As we explore the foundations of companion planting, you'll discover that this method is much more than just placing plants side by side; it's about creating a thriving ecosystem that works in harmony with nature.

Companion planting taps into the subtle yet powerful interactions between plants to create a garden that is not only productive but also resilient and vibrant. By understanding the philosophy behind companion planting and its benefits, you will be equipped to transform your garden into a self-sufficient oasis that is both beautiful and bountiful.

1.1 The Philosophy Behind Companion Planting

Harmony with Nature

The essence of companion planting lies in its core principle: harmony with nature. Unlike conventional gardening practices that often involve synthetic inputs and monocultures, companion planting encourages a diverse mix of plants that support each other's growth and well-being. This approach minimizes the need for chemical fertilizers and pesticides and enhances the garden's natural resilience. By mimicking the diversity in natural ecosystems, companion planting creates a balanced and harmonious environment where plants can thrive just as nature intended.

Historical Roots

The roots of companion planting stretch back thousands of years and span various cultures and continents. Ancient civilizations, including the Native Americans, practised this method long before it was recognized by modern science. One famous example is the "Three Sisters" technique, where corn, beans, and squash are grown together, each plant supporting the others in a seamless symbiosis. Corn provides a structure for the beans to climb; beans fix nitrogen in the soil to nourish the corn, and squash spreads along the ground, blocking the sunlight from weeds. This intelligent setup not only showcases the ingenuity of companion planting but also underscores the role of traditional knowledge in informing and enriching our current gardening practices, connecting us to the roots of gardening.

Community and Biodiversity

At its heart, companion planting is about fostering a sense of community among plants. Each plant supports the others in a companion-planted garden, creating a robust community that is more resistant to pests and diseases. This biodiversity is not only vital to the health of the garden but also to its productivity. Diverse plantings confuse and deter pests while attracting beneficial insects, which help in pollination and pest control. Furthermore, a biodiverse garden is a step towards preserving the ecological balance, contributing positively to the local wildlife and the broader environment.

Symbiotic Relationships

Symbiotic relationships are the cornerstone of effective companion planting. These relationships are built on mutual benefits that plants offer each other. For example, tall sunflowers can provide shade for heat-sensitive lettuce, while marigolds emit a scent that repels pests harmful to tomatoes. Understanding these relationships allows you to place plants to maximise their inherent strengths strategically. This natural method of supporting plant health reduces your garden's dependency on external inputs and increases its yield and vitality.

Visual Element: Companion Planting Chart

Beets	Carrots	Celery	Corn	Cucumbers	Peppers	Potatoes	Squash	Strawberries	Tomatoes
Companions	Companions	Companions	Companions	Companions	Companions	Companions	Companions	Companions	Companions
Carrots	Brassicas	Beans	Beans	Beans	Basil	Celery	Beans pole	Beans bush	Asparagus
Corn	Chives	brasicas	Brasicas	Brasicas	Carrots	Cilantro	Borage	Garlic	Basil
Cucumber	Leeks	Chives	Beets	Chives	Cucumbers	Corn	Corn	Lettuce	Beets
Brassicas	Lettuce	Garlic	Cucumber	Corn	Onions	Garlic	Lettuce	Onions	Chive
Garlic	Onions	Spinach	Dill	Lettuce	Squash	Onions	Marigolds	Peas	Cilantro
Leeks	Radishes	Tomatoes	Marigolds	Marigolds	Tomatoes	Beans bush	Melon	Sage	Cucumbers
Lettuce	Peppers	Leeks	Parsley	Peas	Parsley	Marigolds	Peas	Spinach	Garlic
	Rosemary	cilantro	Peas	Onions	Rosemary		Peppers	Thyme	Lettuce
			Potatoes	Peppers	Peas				Marigolds
			Squash	tomatoes	Oregano				Onions
			Melon	Dill					Parsley
			sunflower	Kale					Peppers
									Sage
Avoid	Avoid	Avoid	Avoid	Avoid	Avoid	Avoid	Avoid	Avoid	Avoid
Dill	Parsnips	Carrots	Celery	Basil	Beans	Asparagus	Brasicas	Brasicas	Brasicas
Pole beans	Potatoes	Parsnips	Tomatoes	Potatoes	Brasicas	Carrots	Potatoes	Fennell	Corn
				Rosemary	Fennel	Cucumbers		kohlrabi	Dill
				Sage		Melon			Kohlrabi
						Sunflowers			Potatoes

Here is a detailed companion planting chart to help you visualize the symbiotic relationships between different plants. This chart outlines which plants benefit from being near each other and which should be kept apart. Use it as a reference when planning your garden layout to ensure optimal plant partnerships.

By embracing these principles, you lay the groundwork for a garden that is not only productive but also harmonious with the natural world. As we continue to explore the various aspects of companion planting, keep in mind that each step forward is a step towards a more sustainable and fulfilling gardening experience, leading to a garden that is not just harmonious but also highly productive and successful.

1.2 Decoding the Science: How Plants Benefit Each Other

Imagine walking through a forest; you're not just seeing a bunch of trees and plants coexisting, but there's an entire conversation happening right beneath the surface and through the air. This isn't science fiction—it's the reality of how plants interact in nature and our gardens. This silent dialogue is crucial in companion planting, where the right plant pairings can significantly amplify each other's health and productivity. Understanding these natural processes allows you to turn your garden into a thriving ecosystem of healthy, productive plants.

Chemical Signaling

Plants are incredible communicators. They can alert neighbours about threats like pests or diseases through chemical signals released into the air or soil. This chemical signalling, known as allelopathy, can sometimes inhibit the growth of nearby plant competitors. Still, a well-planned companion garden plays a beneficial role in mutual protection and growth enhancement. For example, when certain types of sage are planted near cabbage, they release chemicals that repel cabbage moths, a common pest. These signals create an invisible barrier that helps maintain the plants' health without a drop of chemical pesticide.

Root Systems and Nutrient Sharing

Underneath the soil, a complex network of roots forms the foundation of your garden's health. In companion planting, these root systems interact to create a more efficient nutrient and water uptake system. Take the classic partnership of carrots and onions. Carrot roots go deep and can loosen the soil, which benefits onion roots that are more shallow and spread out. This arrangement allows onions to easily access nutrients in the upper soil layers, while carrots can reach minerals from deeper down. The result is healthier plants and better water penetration and retention, ensuring that plants stay hydrated and nourished even during dry spells.

Pest Management

Integrating certain plants can naturally keep pests at bay, a cornerstone of successful companion planting. Marigolds are a popular companion for many vegetable gardens because they contain toxic compounds to nematodes and other soil-borne pests. The fragrance of marigolds is also known to deter aphids and mosquitoes. This method of pest control is not only organic, but it also enhances the garden's overall health, reducing the likelihood of disease and pest infestations that often require chemical solutions. You're setting up a natural defence system that protects your garden's biodiversity by placing the right plants together.

Improved Pollination

The diversity in a companion planted garden also plays a pivotal role in attracting various pollinators, which is essential for garden productivity. It's fascinating how flowers of different shapes and colours lure a wide range of pollinators, ensuring that all plants have a better chance of being pollinated. The variety of nature is truly unique. For instance, planting basil beside tomatoes not only improves the flavour of the tomatoes but also attracts bees, which are vital pollinators for tomato plants. This increased pollinator activity not only boosts the health and yield of your garden but also contributes to the ecological health of your surrounding environment by supporting bee populations.

Each interaction highlights the intricate and intelligent ways plants can support one another. By leveraging the natural capabilities of various plants through thoughtful companion planting, gardeners can create a harmonious and productive garden that requires fewer inputs and gives back more in terms of yield and sustainability. As we continue exploring the layers of companion planting, remember that each plant in your garden plays a role not just in the aesthetics of the space but, more importantly, in the health and balance of a miniature ecosystem. You have the joy and responsibility to nurture.

1.3 Companion Planting Myths vs. Facts

Navigating the world of gardening, particularly companion planting, can sometimes feel like you're wading through a swamp of folklore, half-truths, and outright myths. Separating the wheat from the chaff is crucial, as well as ensuring that your gardening practices are grounded in reality and backed by science. This understanding not only maximizes your garden's potential but also saves you from common pitfalls caused by widespread misconceptions, leaving you feeling enlightened and informed about the true principles of gardening.

Debunking Common Myths

One prevalent myth is that simply placing any two plants together benefits both. While it's tempting to believe that all plants play nicely with each other, the truth is more nuanced. Not all plant interactions are beneficial; some can be downright harmful. For instance, while tomatoes and carrots can be great companions, tomatoes and potatoes—both nightshade family members—can increase each other's susceptibility to blight. This example underscores the importance of not planting indiscriminately and making informed choices about which plants to pair. It's essential to understand that companion planting isn't about magical pairings but strategic placements based on plant biology and chemistry.

Another common misconception is that companion planting can completely replace traditional pest management. While it's true that certain plant combinations can deter specific pests, this method is part of a broader integrated pest management system. For example, marigolds repel nematodes and deter some insects, but they won't protect your garden from all pests. Effective pest management often requires a combination of methods, including physical barriers, biological control agents, and sometimes even organic pesticides, depending on the severity and type of pest infestation.

Real Benefits

Turning to the genuine benefits of companion planting, the advantages extend well beyond pest control. Scientific studies have validated that certain plant combinations can improve soil health, enhance nutrient uptake, and boost crop yields. For example, the classic combination of corn, beans, and squash, known as the Three Sisters, demonstrates a symbiotic relationship where each plant contributes to a healthier garden ecosystem. The beans fix nitrogen in the soil, benefiting the nitrogen-loving corn, while the squash acts as a living mulch, conserving moisture and suppressing weeds. These tangible and measurable benefits highlight the potential for companion planting to create more efficient and sustainable gardening systems.

Moreover, companion planting contributes to biodiversity, which has been shown to enhance ecosystem resilience. A diverse garden attracts various beneficial insects and pollinators, which helps with pest control and improves pollination, leading to better fruit and seed production. This increase in biodiversity can transform a garden from a static collection of plants into a dynamic ecosystem teeming with life.

Limitations

However, it's essential to acknowledge that companion planting has limitations and is not a one-size-fits-all solution. The effectiveness of companion planting can vary significantly depending on factors such as climate, soil type, and plant varieties. For example, what works well in a temperate climate may not be suitable for a tropical environment. Additionally, the benefits of companion planting may take several seasons to become apparent, requiring patience and persistence from the gardener. Understanding these limitations is crucial for setting realistic expectations and adapting strategies to fit specific garden conditions.

Best Practices

To navigate these complexities, here are some best practices for implementing effective companion planting strategies in your garden. First, start small and observe. Choose a few well-documented plant pairings and monitor their progress throughout the season. This approach lets you gather firsthand insights into what works and doesn't in your garden environment. Second, keep detailed records of plant combinations, weather conditions, pest activity, and crop yields. This data will be invaluable as you refine your companion planting strategies.

Additionally, it's wise to consult with local gardeners and agricultural extensions, as they can offer region-specific advice often grounded in years of experience and observation. Finally, be flexible and willing to adapt. Gardening is an ongoing experiment, and what works one year may not work the next due to changes in weather patterns, pest populations, or other environmental factors.

By approaching companion planting with a curious and scientific mindset, you can maximize its benefits while minimizing disappointments. This method offers a fascinating glimpse into the complex interactions within your garden and invites you to engage more deeply with the natural world. As you continue to learn and experiment, remember that each step forward enriches your garden and your experience as a gardener.

1.4 Creating Your First Companion Plant Pairing

Selecting the perfect companions for your garden is like setting up a good dinner party. You want to pair individuals who will get along well, enhance each other's best qualities, and ensure everyone leaves happier and healthier than when they arrived. The same goes for plants. When kicking off your companion planting adventure, the first step is choosing plant pairs that coexist and mutually benefit from each other's company. This involves understanding each plant's unique needs and strengths, ensuring they align to create a thriving garden ecosystem.

When selecting companion plants, consider their nutrient needs, growth patterns, and pest resistance qualities. For instance, some plants, like beans, are known as nitrogen-fixers, meaning they pull nitrogen from the air and fix it into the soil, enriching it for neighbouring plants that might be heavy nitrogen feeders like corn. Other considerations include differing root depths, which ensures they aren't competing for the same resources below the soil. Shallow-rooted herbs can happily thrive alongside deeper-rooted vegetables. Pairing fast-growing plants with slower-growing varieties is also beneficial, allowing the quick growers to shade the soil and reduce weed growth around their slower companions.

Start with tried and tested pairings for beginners eager to see positive results. Marigolds and almost any garden vegetable make good partners; they are not only pretty but also repel many pests and attract beneficial insects. Tomatoes and basil are another great duo; not only do they go well together in sauces, but planting basil alongside your tomatoes can help repel flies and mosquitoes, and some gardeners swear it improves the flavour of their tomatoes. These simple starter pairings are easy to manage, provide clear benefits, and boost your confidence as you see your garden flourish.

Once you've made your plant selections and set them in the soil, the real magic—and science—begins. Observing how your plant pairs interact is crucial. Sometimes, despite your best efforts, certain plants won't get along, and that's okay. It's part of the learning process. Pay attention to signs of distress, such as stunted growth or increased pest activity. These could be indications that your plant pairings aren't ideal. Adjustment is a natural part of gardening. You might find that moving plants to different locations within the garden or adjusting their watering schedule can make a difference. Remember, flexibility is a vital trait of any successful gardener.

Keeping a garden journal can be an invaluable tool in this process. Note your plant pairings, their locations, and any observations about their growth, health, and the presence of pests or diseases. Recording these details will help you track the progress and conditions of your current garden and provide insights for future planting seasons. Over time, this journal will become a personalized guide filled with your own observations and experiences tailored to your specific garden conditions and local climate. It's a living document that grows richer and more helpful with each passing season.

As you experiment with different combinations and configurations, you'll likely discover pairings uniquely suited to your garden's microclimate and your preferences. These successes are not just rewarding in terms of yield but are also deeply satisfying on a personal level, as they reflect your growth and learning as a gardener. So, keep curious, stay observant, and remember that every season brings new opportunities for learning and development in companion planting.

1.5 The Role of Pollinators in Companion Planting

When you wander through your garden, pausing to admire the dance of a butterfly or the industrious buzz of a bee, you're witnessing more than a mere spectacle of nature; you're observing crucial contributors to your garden's success. Pollinators, including bees, butterflies, moths, and even some birds and bats, play an essential role in the life cycle of many plants. In the context of companion planting, understanding how to attract and support these vital creatures can dramatically enhance the productivity and health of your garden.

Attracting Pollinators

Introducing attractive plants to these creatures is the first step in creating a pollinator-friendly garden. Flowers with bright colours and strong fragrances are usually the most effective at drawing in pollinators. For instance, lavender and borage are favourites among bees for their abundant nectar, while butterflies are often drawn to the vibrant blooms of zinnias and marigolds. However, it's not just about picking the right flowers. The layout of your garden can also impact its attractiveness to pollinators. Grouping flowering plants in swathes rather than dotting them individually allows for easier feeding and can create a more appealing target for pollinators from a distance.

Moreover, the diversity of plant species in a companion planting setup can provide pollinators with a broader range of nutritional options, which is crucial for their health and survival. Mixing flowers of different shapes and sizes ensures that various pollinators, each with unique feeding preferences and habits, find something in your garden that suits their needs. This helps attract pollinators and extends their stay in your garden, increasing the chances of pollination.

Supporting Pollinator Health

Beyond just attracting these helpful creatures, it's vital to consider their overall health and well-being, which in turn affects the health of your garden. Diverse plantings provide not only food but also habitats for pollinators. Many insects, including beneficial ones, need shelter for nesting or protection against predators. Plants like sunflowers and tall grasses can offer these safe havens where pollinators can rest or hide. Additionally, avoiding pesticides or opting for natural pest control methods is critical. Chemicals that kill garden pests can also harm pollinators, so maintaining a balance is vital. Using natural pest deterrents, such as garlic or chilli spray, or simply encouraging the presence of predator insects like ladybugs can help keep pest populations in check without endangering pollinators.

Seasonal Considerations

To support pollinators throughout the growing season, it's essential to plant a succession of blooms that ensure continuous food availability. Spring bulbs like crocuses and daffodils provide early nectar sources when food is scarce. Following these, your main season crops and flowers take over, and later in the season, plants like asters and goldenrods can offer sustenance to pollinators preparing for winter. This strategy supports a healthy pollinator population and contributes to a vibrant and productive garden from spring to fall.

1.6 Understanding Companion Planting Zones

Navigating our gardens' diverse climates and geographies is much like dressing appropriately for the weather. Certain plants are better suited to specific climates and locations, just as you wouldn't wear flip-flops in a snowstorm. By understanding how to tailor your companion planting strategies to your local conditions, you can optimize the health and productivity of your garden. This isn't just about knowing your frost dates or annual rainfall; it's about becoming attuned to the rhythms of your local ecosystem and working in harmony with them.

Climate and Geography

Every region presents unique gardening challenges and opportunities. What thrives in the humid Southeast might struggle in the arid Southwest. Therefore, tailoring your companion planting strategy to your specific climate and geography is crucial. This means considering sunlight intensity, humidity levels, and average temperatures. For example, maximizing sunlight exposure is critical to cooler northern climates, so you might place taller plants slightly to the north of shorter companions to avoid shading them. In hotter regions, however, creating shade is often necessary, and companion plants like tall sunflowers can relieve more heat-sensitive plants like lettuce.

Considering your garden area's wind patterns and topography is also beneficial. Windbreaks, such as rows of bushes or trellises with climbing vines, can protect delicate plants from harsh winds. Similarly, understanding your garden's slope can help manage water drainage and erosion. Companion plants with deep root systems can be strategically placed on slopes to help stabilize the soil and assist in water absorption, reducing runoff and soil loss.

Hardiness Zones

Understanding and utilizing hardiness zones is another crucial element in selecting the right plants for your garden. Hardiness zones, developed by the USDA, are based on a region's average minimum winter temperatures and are a great starting point for determining which plants are most likely to thrive in your locale. Each plant variety has a recommended zone range, and sticking to these recommendations can significantly increase your gardening success.

However, it's not just about survival through the winter. Some plants need a certain amount of cold to trigger dormancy or to set buds for the next season's growth. Others might need a more extended, warm period to reach maturity. Knowing your area's hardiness zone, you can make informed choices about what plants to select as main crops and companions. For instance, if you're gardening in a zone that experiences mild winters, you might choose citrus trees as a backdrop to a bed of heat-loving herbs like basil and thyme, which not only enjoy similar conditions but also can benefit from the shelter provided by the trees.

Microclimates

Conditions can vary dramatically even within a single garden. These variations create what are known as microclimates, and they can be influenced by factors such as proximity to buildings, bodies of water, or specific types of paving or mulching materials. By learning to identify and utilize these microclimates, you can expand the variety of plants you grow and increase the effectiveness of your companion planting strategies.

For example, the south side of a fence or building typically receives more heat and light and is protected from northern winds, making it a prime spot for plants that require more warmth and shelter. Conversely, an area shaded by a large tree might be perfect for growing cool-season vegetables like spinach or peas, which might otherwise bolt in too much sun. Observing these microclimates throughout the year gives you a powerful tool for placing companion plants in locations where they can best support each other's growth.

Adapting Over Time

Remember that these conditions can change as you become more attuned to the specifics of your garden's climate and microclimates. Climate patterns can shift, and garden structures might alter microclimates. Trees grow larger and cast more shade, new buildings might block wind or reflect heat, and changes in neighbouring properties can affect your garden conditions.

Flexibility is your greatest ally. What works one year might not work the next, and being open to observing these changes and adapting your strategies is critical. This might mean swapping out plant varieties, altering your garden layout, or experimenting with new companion planting combinations. Each season's successes and challenges provide valuable lessons that can refine your approach, making you not just a gardener but a keen observer of the natural world.

By embracing these principles, you position yourself to work with your garden's unique characteristics, leading to a healthier, more productive environment. This thoughtful approach, grounded in understanding your local conditions, ensures that your garden is a place of beauty and productivity and a reflection of the ecosystem in which it resides.

TWO

Planning Your Companion Garden

As you turn the soil and dream about the possibilities, remember that every inch of your garden holds potential, much like a blank canvas waiting for a painter's touch. Planning your companion garden is an exhilarating step in your gardening adventure—where your creativity and the lessons from nature intersect to create something truly magical. Let's roll up our sleeves and consider using every square foot effectively, not just for this season, but as a foundation for future growth and abundance.

2.1 Assessing Your Space

First, understanding your gardening space's physical and environmental characteristics is crucial. Start by observing the amount of sunlight different areas receive throughout the day; this will be a critical factor in deciding where to place various plants since some need full sun while others thrive in partial shade. Next, get up close and personal with your soil. Dig in, feel its texture, and consider getting a soil test from your local extension service to learn about nutrient levels and pH. Water availability is another critical factor—note where water collects after rain and which areas remain dry. These initial observations will provide a roadmap for what can be planted, ensuring that each plant's needs are met.

For instance, if you have a moist sunny spot, it's perfect for moisture-loving sun worshippers like mint or cucumber. On the other hand, a dry, sunny area could be an excellent spot for Mediterranean herbs such as rosemary and thyme, which prefer less water and more heat. Understanding these nuances lets you make the most of your garden's unique environmental mosaic.

Maximizing Small Areas

Not everyone has expansive yards, and that's perfectly okay! With ingenuity, smaller spaces and balconies can become lush, productive gardens. Vertical gardening and container planting are your best friends here. Vertical gardening uses trellises, wall planters, and even hanging baskets to grow upwards, making the most of vertical space. Plants like beans, peas, and vine tomatoes adore climbing and add a touch of verdant beauty to any vertical structure.

Container planting, on the other hand, is wonderfully versatile. Almost any vegetable, herb, or flower that grows in a garden can be grown in a container. Choose containers large enough to accommodate the full-size plant and have good drainage. Containers are also great for experimenting with different soil types and mixes, as you can tailor the soil precisely to the needs of specific plants without affecting the rest of your garden.

Optimizing Layout

The layout of your companion garden can significantly impact its success. When arranging plants, consider their sunlight and soil needs and how they can benefit each other. Plant tall sunflowers on the north side of shorter crops to provide shade and wind protection without blocking their sunlight. Use aromatic herbs like lavender and rosemary around the edges of your garden to help deter pests with their strong scents.

Furthermore, think about how your plants will be accessed for harvesting and maintenance. Create pathways that allow easy access to all plants without the risk of stepping on growing beds. This makes gardening more enjoyable and protects plants from being compacted by foot traffic, which can affect their growth.

Future Expansion

Even if you're starting small, it's wise to think about the future scalability of your garden. As you become more experienced, you might want to expand or diversify your plantings. Plan your current garden layout with expansion in mind. Perhaps leave space for additional beds or containers, or start with a modular garden design that can easily be scaled up. Planning for future growth makes the expansion easier and keeps you inspired and forward-thinking in your gardening journey.

Interactive Element: Garden Planning Exercise

To implement these ideas, here's an exercise to help you visualize and plan your space. Draw a simple map of your garden area and mark the different light and moisture zones based on your observations. Use this map to sketch where plants might go according to their sunlight, soil, and water needs. Consider access paths and how you might expand in the future. This exercise requires no artistic skill—simple sketches and notes are all you need. It's a practical tool to transform your observations into a concrete plan, setting a solid foundation for your thriving companion garden.

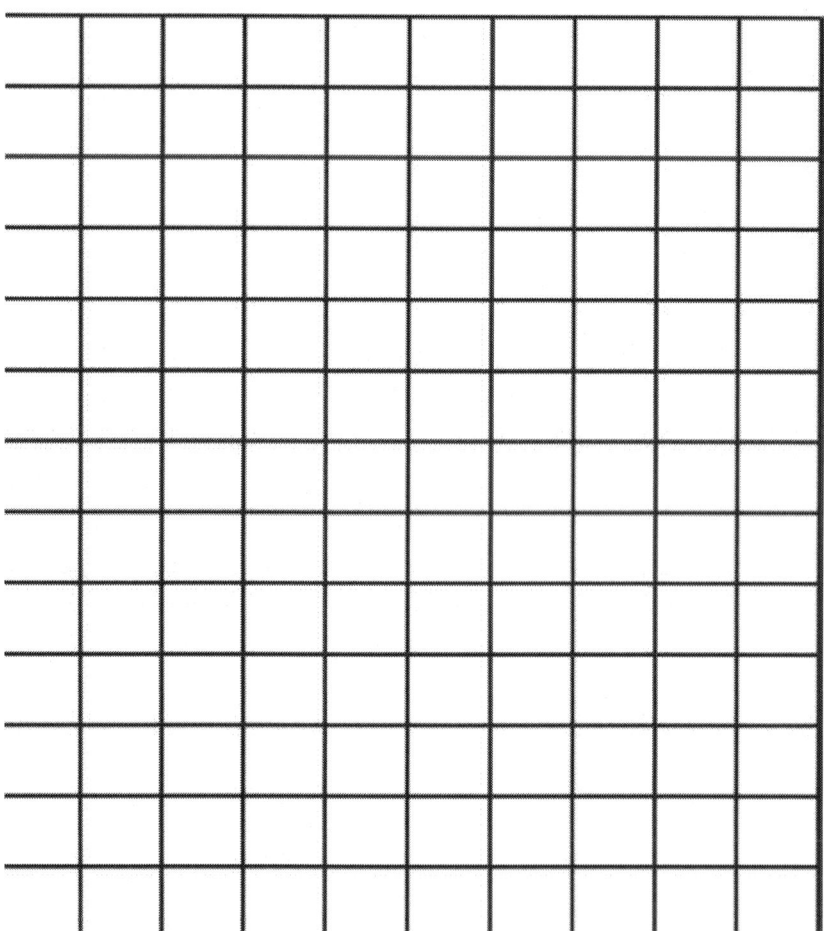

2.2 Designing Your Companion Planting Layout

Creating a companion planting layout that is as functional as it is beautiful can be compared to crafting a detailed painting where each brushstroke contributes to a larger, harmonious picture. The first step in this creative process is drawing your garden plan, which acts as a blueprint and a guide for your gardening endeavours. Start with a precise, scaled drawing of your garden space. Use graph paper or a gardening app to map the area, marking key features such as existing trees, paths, and buildings. This map becomes the foundation for building your companion planting strategy.

As you sketch, consider the relationships between different plants and how their interactions could benefit one another. For example, tall plants that love the sun can be placed on the north side of shorter, shade-tolerant plants to prevent them from casting shadows. Group plants with similar water and nutrient needs together to simplify care and maximize efficiency. This thoughtful placement ensures that each plant supports its neighbours, leading to a healthier and more productive garden. Your plan should also include space for walkways to allow easy access for maintenance and harvesting without disturbing the plants. As you draw, remember that this plan isn't set in stone—it's a living document that can evolve as you learn more about your garden's unique needs and the dynamics of your plant interactions.

Rotational planting is another critical element of your garden design strategy, especially for maintaining soil health and controlling pests naturally. This technique involves changing the location of specific plant types in your garden each year. For example, moving nightshades like tomatoes and peppers to a different bed can prevent soil-borne diseases such as blight from taking hold, as many pathogens accumulate when the same crop is planted in the same soil year after year. Rotational planting also helps in managing nutrient depletion. Legumes, for instance, fix nitrogen in the soil, which can benefit leafy greens planted in the same spot the following year. By rotating crops, you ensure that soil nutrients are used and replenished balanced, reducing the need for chemical fertilizers and enhancing your garden's overall sustainability.

Incorporating aesthetics and accessibility into your garden design makes the space more enjoyable and functional. Arrange plants not only for their compatibility but also for their colours and textures, creating a visually pleasing array. Consider the view from inside your home or the places where you like to sit and relax in your garden. Place eye-catching plants like sunflowers or colourful swaths of blooming perennials in these areas to enhance your enjoyment of the space. Accessibility is equally essential—ensure that paths are wide enough to accommodate a wheelbarrow or garden cart, and consider raised beds or container gardens for easier access, especially if bending and kneeling are challenging. These practical considerations make gardening less of a chore and a pleasure, encouraging you to spend more time in your outdoor sanctuary.

Perennials play a crucial role in your garden's long-term stability and health. Unlike annuals, which need to be replanted each year, perennials come back season after season, providing a reliable structure to your garden. When integrating perennials into your companion planting layout, choose plants that will thrive in your climate and support the needs of surrounding annuals. For instance, perennial herbs like sage and thyme can deter pests while providing culinary benefits. Larger perennials, such as rhubarb or asparagus, can serve as focal points in your garden design, around which you can rotate annual crops. Including perennials in your garden adds variety and interest and contributes to creating a diverse ecosystem that supports a wide range of wildlife, from pollinators to beneficial insects. By planning to include these hardy plants, you ensure a resilient garden that grows in beauty and productivity year after year.

2.3 Companion Plants for Small Spaces and Balconies

When you think about gardening, do you picture vast rows of crops stretching out under the sky? Let's shift that image a bit.

Imagine lush green spaces bustling with life, thriving on your balcony or in a cosy patio corner. Small spaces and balconies are full of untapped planting potential, and with the right approach, they can transform into mini gardens that yield a surprising amount of produce and beauty. The key here lies in selecting plants that love the container life and complement each other in such settings.

Container gardening is a fantastic way to manage your planting environment exactly as each species likes. Some plants, like herbs and strawberries, are natural for containers because they can be controlled quickly and don't require deep soil to flourish. When pairing plants for containers, consider their growth habits and needs. For example, tomatoes do wonderfully in deep containers but also need a lot of sunlight and air circulation. Pairing them with basil, which thrives under the same conditions and can benefit from the shade the tomato plants provide when they get bushy, creates a mini ecosystem where both plants can thrive. Additionally, the basil helps repel insects that might otherwise be tempted by the tomatoes, demonstrating how companion planting in containers can mimic the beneficial relationships found in more extensive gardens.

Another aspect to consider is the soil and feeding needs. While carrots and radishes grow well in deeper pots, they have different nutrient needs. Carrots are heavier feeders than radishes, so combining them in the same container might result in one outcompeting the other. Instead, pair radishes with spinach, which has similar light and water requirements but does not compete for the same nutrients. This thoughtful pairing ensures that both plants can grow without hindrance, maximizing the yield from your container garden.

Vertical gardening is another ingenious way to make the most of limited space. Utilizing vertical space effectively can double or even triple your planting area, which is particularly useful on small balconies or compact patios. Climbing plants such as peas, beans, and even some varieties of squash and melons can be trained to grow up trellises, saving ground space for other crops. But it's not just about going upwards. Think about layering—lower-growing plants prefer shade that can be placed beneath these vertical growers, creating a living green wall. For instance, lettuces, which tend to bolt and turn bitter in too much heat, can thrive in a cool, moist environment under a canopy of climbing cucumbers or beans.

Proper watering and maintenance are critical in these confined gardening setups. Containers and vertical planters can dry out much faster than traditional garden beds, especially in warm, windy weather. To manage this, consider self-watering containers, which include a reservoir at the bottom that allows plants to absorb moisture as needed. This system conserves water and ensures that plants receive moisture consistently, crucial for stress-free growth. Regular feeding is also essential, as containerized plants can quickly exhaust nutrients in their soil. Use a balanced, organic liquid fertilizer every few weeks to keep your plants healthy and productive.

Now, let's draw inspiration from a few success stories that illustrate the power of small-space companion planting. Picture a vibrant balcony garden where trailing nasturtiums, known for their bright, edible flowers, cascade over the sides of a container that houses bush beans. The nasturtiums deter pests that might otherwise target the beans, while the height of the bean plants provides a bit of shade, keeping the nasturtiums cool and vibrant. Another example is a vertical setup where sweet peas climb a trellis, their roots intermingling in the soil with carrots. The sweet peas help loosen the soil, making it easier for the carrots to grow deep and robust. In another container, chives and strawberries share space; the chives help ward off insects while the strawberries provide ground cover, reducing the need for weeding.

These examples show container and vertical gardens can be highly productive, stunningly beautiful, and immensely satisfying to cultivate. Whether you are managing a small balcony or a modest patio area, the principles of companion planting can be applied to create a lush, productive, and sustainable garden. By choosing the right plants and understanding their needs, even the smallest spaces can yield an abundance of herbs, vegetables, and flowers, bringing the joy of gardening to any home, regardless of size.

2.4 Seasonal Planning for Year-Round Harvests

Imagine your garden thriving through the rolling seasons, each month bringing its own unique bounty. This consistent harvest isn't just a stroke of luck; it's the result of strategic planning and understanding the rhythms of nature. Seasonal planning is vital in turning your garden into a year-round source of fresh produce, and the key to this is mastering the art of succession planting. Succession planting involves staggering the planting of crops to ensure that as one crop finishes, another begins, providing a continuous supply of vegetables and herbs. For instance, after harvesting spring radishes, the same space can be immediately replanted with heat-loving basil or beans that thrive in the summer warmth. This method not only maximizes the use of your garden space but also keeps the soil active and your kitchen well-stocked.

To get started, you'll want to create a planting calendar. List the vegetables you want to grow, noting their growth cycle from seed to harvest. Then, stagger their planting dates based on these cycles. You can plan several plantings for quick-growing crops like lettuce and spinach, spaced 2-3 weeks apart. For longer-growing vegetables, like tomatoes or pumpkins, consider their peak harvesting time and what other crops could follow once harvested. This ongoing cycle ensures a regular supply of fresh produce and covers your soil, which can help prevent weeds and soil erosion.

As you dive deeper into seasonal planning, another crucial aspect to consider is extending the growing season beyond the usual limits of your climate zone. This can be particularly rewarding, allowing you to enjoy fresh greens even as the first frosts arrive. Techniques like using cold frames, essentially mini-greenhouses, can protect your crops from early autumn or late spring frosts, giving you a few extra weeks of harvesting. Similarly, greenhouses can provide a controlled environment for growing more plants through the colder months. These structures capture and hold heat during the day, keeping the air and soil warm enough to sustain plant growth even when outside temperatures drop.

Moreover, starting seeds indoors can be a game-changer for those looking to get a head start on the growing season. By sowing seeds in seed trays or pots inside your home and gradually acclimating them to outdoor conditions—a process known as hardening off—you can have robust seedlings ready to transplant as soon as the weather warms. This method not only extends the growing season but also improves the survival rate of young plants, as they are protected from the variable conditions outdoors during their most vulnerable stages.

As the colder months approach, your garden needs a different kind of attention. Winter planning involves harvesting the last autumn crops and preparing your garden for the cold. Selecting winter-hardy plants like kale, Brussels sprouts, and certain herbs can keep your garden productive and vibrant, even in frosty conditions. Also, mulching provides a protective blanket for your soil, preserving moisture and insulating plant roots from freezing temperatures. Mulch made from organic materials like straw or leaves also breaks down over time, adding nutrients back into the soil, which enhances its fertility for the next planting season.

Crop rotation is another cornerstone of maintaining a healthy garden throughout the year. This practice involves changing the types of crops grown in a particular garden area each year. It helps prevent the buildup of pests and diseases when the same crop is grown repeatedly in the same soil. For example, following tomatoes with a leafy green like spinach can help break the life cycle of soil-borne diseases that target nightshades. Furthermore, crop rotation can aid in managing soil fertility. Following a heavy feeder like corn with a nitrogen-fixing legume such as beans can help replenish the nitrogen the corn uses, maintaining a balance that keeps your soil healthy and productive.

Implementing these seasonal strategies requires planning and flexibility, but the rewards are plentiful. With a garden that adapts to each season, you can enjoy the fruits of your labour all year round, making every part of the gardening season a time of abundance and joy. Whether it's the lush growth of summer vegetables or the crisp harvest of autumn roots, your garden can become a testament to the beauty and productivity of nature in every season.

2.5 Water Management in Companion Planting

When you envision a thriving garden, the image is often drenched in sunlight, but let's not overlook another vital ingredient: water. Managing water in a companion garden isn't just about making sure your plants get enough water. It's about using water wisely and sustainably, ensuring every drop supports your garden's health and productivity. From innovative irrigation techniques to strategic mulching, let's explore how you can optimize water use in your companion garden.

Irrigation might sound technical, but it's essentially about getting water to where it's needed most without waste. The key here is efficiency. Drip irrigation, for instance, is a fantastic system that delivers water directly to the soil at the base of your plants. This method minimizes evaporation and runoff, ensuring that water goes directly to your plant's roots where needed most. It's convenient in a companion planting setup where plants with varying water needs live side by side. With drip irrigation, you can adjust water flow to meet the specific needs of each plant or plant group. For example, your thirsty tomatoes can receive more frequent watering, while nearby herbs that prefer drier soil, like rosemary and thyme, get less. This targeted watering conserves water and prevents the stress from over- or under-watering, keeping your plants healthy and happy.

Another effective technique is to use a soaker, a porous hose laid out along the ground. These hoses let water seep into the soil, hydrating plants gradually and deeply. This is especially beneficial for deep-rooted plants in your companion garden, encouraging them to grow deeper roots, which help them access water more efficiently and become more drought-resistant. When setting up soaker hoses, weave them through your garden beds near the plants' base, ensuring even water distribution across different plant types. This method is water- and time-efficient, reducing the need for frequent manual watering.

Mulching is another critical strategy in water management. Covering the soil with mulch can significantly reduce water evaporation from the soil surface, which is particularly important during hot weather. Organic mulches like straw, bark, or leaf mould are great for retaining moisture; they also break down over time, adding nutrients to the soil and improving its structure. When applying mulch, spread a layer about 2-3 inches thick around your plants, being careful not to pile it too close to plant stems to avoid rot. This layer acts like a blanket, keeping the soil cool and moist and providing your plants with a stable environment even during temperature fluctuations. Additionally, mulch helps suppress weeds that compete with your plants for water, making your garden more water-efficient and easier to maintain.

Choosing drought-tolerant plant pairings can significantly affect regions where water scarcity is a concern. Plants like lavender and sedum naturally adapt to dry conditions and can thrive with minimal watering. When paired in a garden, these plants form a resilient landscape that requires less frequent watering. Companion planting these drought-tolerant varieties with similarly hardy plants not. It only creates a garden that is more likely to succeed in arid climates but also conserves water, a crucial consideration in sustainable gardening practices.

Lastly, capturing and utilizing rainwater can be a game-changer in managing garden hydration sustainably. Setting up a rain barrel system to collect rainwater from your roof is a simple yet effective way to reduce your reliance on municipal water systems and make the most of natural rainfall. This collected water can be used for irrigation, especially during dry spells, providing your garden with a free, plentiful water source. Rainwater is often softer and free of the salts and chemicals in tap water, which can be better for your garden's soil and plants. Using rainwater helps your garden thrive and contributes to a broader environmental effort to conserve and respect our water resources.

Integrating these water management strategies into your companion planting plan will ensure that your garden remains lush and productive and contribute to water conservation efforts.

Remember, every drop counts, and with suitable approaches, you can make every drop work effectively for your garden's benefit.

2.6 Sunlight and Shade: Maximizing Photosynthesis

Sunlight, the lifeblood of your garden, plays a pivotal role in the growth and health of your plants. Understanding the light requirements of different plants is essential for optimizing Photosynthesis, the process by which plants convert light energy into chemical energy. It's not just about ensuring that plants get enough light; it's about getting the right kind of light at the right time. Some plants revel in full sun, soaking up six or more hours of direct sunlight daily, while others flourish in the subtle dappled light under a canopy or in the gentle morning sun followed by afternoon shade.

Let's start by categorizing your plants based on their sunlight needs. Like most vegetables and flowers, full-sun plants require at least six hours of direct sun daily to thrive. These are your sun worshipers; think tomatoes, peppers, and sunflowers. Part-sun or part-shade plants, such as certain herbs and leafy greens, perform well with about three to six hours of sun, preferably in the cooler hours of the morning. Then, the shade-tolerant species—hostas, ferns, and astilbe, for example—can thrive with less than three hours of direct sunlight each day.

Incorporating shade-tolerant companions into your garden design can help you make the most of areas that receive less sunlight. These plants survive and thrive in lower light, perfect for north-facing gardens or the shadowy spaces beneath taller plants. By understanding which plants need less light, you can effectively utilize every part of your garden, turning what might seem like a limitation into a lush, vibrant planting area.

Harnessing reflection is another ingenious way to maximize light in your garden, especially in areas that might naturally receive less direct sunlight. Reflective surfaces can redirect sunlight to these shadier parts. Consider placing reflective mulches like silver plastic or simple aluminium foil under plants to bounce additional light upwards. Painting walls or fences white or using reflective garden art can also help increase the overall light levels, providing a subtle boost to photosynthesis without direct sun.

Using taller plants as natural sunscreens can protect more delicate, sun-sensitive companions from harsh midday rays. This strategy prevents sunburn on sensitive plants like lettuce, which can bolt or scorch in too much heat and create a microclimate of cooler, moist air beneath the leafy canopy. For example, planting taller sunflowers or corn on the western side of smaller, less sun-tolerant plants can shield them from the intense afternoon sun, ensuring that all your plants receive the benefits of sunlight without the stress.

By thoughtfully assessing and managing the light in your garden, you can create a diverse landscape that supports a wide range of plants. This not only maximizes the productivity and health of your garden but also enhances its beauty, offering a variety of textures and colours that change with the light throughout the day. Whether through the strategic placement of plants or the creative use of reflective materials, optimizing light in your garden is a crucial step towards a successful and sustainable gardening practice.

As this chapter concludes, we've journeyed through understanding the critical roles of sunlight and shade in your garden's ecosystem. From recognizing the specific light requirements of various plants to employing creative strategies to optimize light exposure, each step is designed to enhance the photosynthesis process essential for plant health and productivity. By integrating these insights into your garden planning, you can craft a thriving garden that makes the most of every light source available, ensuring robust growth and vibrant displays.

The next chapter will build on these foundational strategies, guiding you through the integration of advanced planting techniques and care tips that cater to the unique needs of your garden setup. This progression ensures your garden starts strong and continues flourishing, adapting to changes and growing with you.

THREE

Plant Pairings and Their Benefits

I magine stepping into a garden where each plant not only thrives but also contributes to the vitality of its neighbours. This isn't just a place of growth; it's a vibrant tableau of mutual support and cooperation. This chapter delves into the world of specific plant pairings, starting with one of the garden's favourites: tomatoes. Tomatoes are like the friendly neighbours who bring everyone together at a block party; they're central to the garden community, and when paired correctly, they help the entire garden flourish.

3.1 The Best Companion Plants for Tomatoes

Tomatoes are a garden staple and remarkably cooperative in the plant world. They thrive when surrounded by a supportive cast of companion plants that enhance their growth and protect them from pests. Let's explore beneficial relationships, identify the antagonists to avoid, and understand how tomatoes can share nutrients effectively with their garden companions.

Natural Allies

When it comes to enhancing the health and productivity of tomatoes, several plants come to the forefront as ideal companions. Basil is a classic pairing with tomatoes, not just in the kitchen but in the garden, too. This aromatic herb is said to improve the flavour of tomatoes growing nearby and is also reputed to repel flies and mosquitoes. Another great ally is Marigold. Planting marigolds around your tomatoes can help repel nematodes and other pests, thanks to their roots' natural compounds and bright, distracting flowers.

But the benefits don't stop at pest control. Calendula, often called pot marigold, attracts a plethora of beneficial insects, such as ladybugs and hoverflies, which help keep pest populations in check. These insects are attracted to calendula's vibrant flowers, and once they're in your garden, they help to protect all your plants, including tomatoes. Additionally, planting carrots alongside tomatoes can help loosen the soil, allowing tomato roots to penetrate deeper and access more nutrients. This pairing not only optimizes the use of space but also promotes a healthier root system for both plants.

Avoiding Antagonists

While companion planting often focuses on the positive, knowing which plants can harm your tomatoes is crucial. For instance, it is wise to keep tomatoes away from cabbage and relatives (like broccoli, Brussels sprouts, and cauliflower). These plants can stunt the growth of tomatoes by competing for similar nutrients too aggressively. Another less-than-ideal companion is corn, which shares common pests with tomatoes, such as the tomato fruitworm, which can also be a corn earworm.

Nutrient Sharing

Understanding how plants share or compete for nutrients can significantly influence your planting strategy. Tomatoes are heavy feeders, needing a rich supply of nutrients to produce their best fruit. Companion planting with legumes such as beans or peas can be beneficial here. These legumes fix nitrogen in the soil, which tomatoes can readily use for their growth. This natural fertilization helps to maintain soil fertility without the need for chemical fertilizers, making your garden more sustainable and your tomatoes more flourishing.

Pollinator Attraction

Attracting pollinators is critical to maximizing tomato yields. While tomatoes are primarily self-pollinating, bees can help increase pollination rates, producing more plentiful and consistent fruit. Flowers like borage are fantastic at attracting bees and other pollinators. Borage also has the benefit of deterring tomato hornworms, a common pest. By integrating these pollinator-friendly plants into your tomato beds, you not only enhance your tomato yield but also support the pollinators' health, contributing to the overall biodiversity of your garden.

Visual Element: Companion Planting Chart for Tomatoes

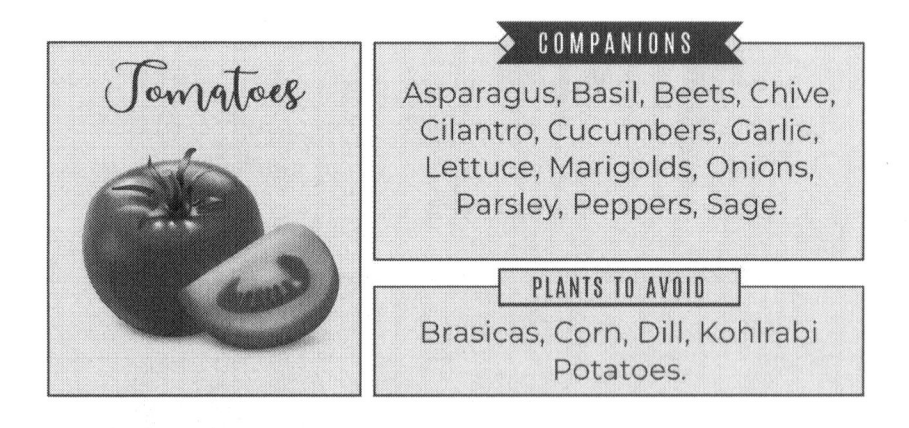

Tomatoes	COMPANIONS
	Asparagus, Basil, Beets, Chive, Cilantro, Cucumbers, Garlic, Lettuce, Marigolds, Onions, Parsley, Peppers, Sage.
	PLANTS TO AVOID
	Brasicas, Corn, Dill, Kohlrabi Potatoes.

Here's a handy chart to help you visualize the best and worst tomato companions. This visual guide makes it easy to reference which plants to grow together and which to keep apart, ensuring your tomatoes have the best environment to thrive.

By choosing the right companions for your tomatoes, you create a garden that is not only more productive but also more resilient. This symbiotic approach to planting encourages a natural balance in the ecosystem, reducing the need for chemical interventions and promoting a healthier, more sustainable garden environment.

As you implement these strategies, observe the interactions in your garden and enjoy creating a thriving plant community where each member brings something valuable to the table.

3.2 Nurturing Your Soil: Nitrogen-Fixing Plant Partners

Diving into soil health, it's clear that nurturing your garden's foundation is as vital as caring for the plants above. One of the most natural and effective ways to enhance soil fertility is through the strategic use of nitrogen-fixing plants, primarily legumes. These incredible plants have the unique ability to capture nitrogen from the air and convert it into a form that's accessible not only to themselves but also to neighbouring plants. This process, facilitated by symbiotic bacteria in their root nodules, enriches the soil, reducing the need for synthetic fertilizers and fostering a more sustainable garden ecosystem.

Legumes like peas, beans, and clovers are suitable for your soil and fantastic companions for various plants. For instance, planting clover in your orchard can boost fruit trees' natural nitrogen, enhancing their growth and fruit production without chemical inputs. Similarly, interplanting beans in your vegetable garden can help other crops thrive by improving soil fertility. These legumes also attract beneficial insects and can serve as a living mulch, covering the soil and helping maintain its moisture and temperature, benefiting their plant neighbours.

Rotating these nitrogen-fixers with other crops can bring long-term benefits to your garden. This practice helps break pest and disease cycles, as many pests and diseases are plant-specific. By changing what's planted in a particular area each season, you can naturally disrupt the life cycles of these garden nuisances, leading to a healthier soil ecosystem. Additionally, rotation allows the soil to recover and maintain its fertility. For instance, after harvesting a heavy-feeding crop like corn, planting a nitrogen-fixing cover crop like vetch can replenish the nutrients used by the corn, preparing the soil for the next planting season. This keeps your soil rich and ready to support whatever you grow next.

When selecting legumes and their companions, consider their compatibility and the specific needs of your garden. For example, beans pair well with corn and squash in a classic "Three Sisters" setup, where each plant supports the others in various ways. The corn provides a natural trellis for the beans to climb, the beans fix nitrogen in the soil, benefiting the nutrient-hungry corn and squash, and the squash's broad leaves shade the soil, helping to retain moisture and suppress weeds. Another excellent pairing is peas and carrots; the peas enrich the soil with nitrogen, which carrots, being heavy feeders, greatly appreciate. These pairings optimize space and resources and enhance your garden's productivity and health.

Beyond nitrogen fixation, maintaining soil health involves regularly adding organic matter and ensuring proper soil structure. Composting is an excellent way to recycle kitchen and garden waste into rich, nutrient-filled organic matter that can significantly benefit your soil. Regularly adding compost to your garden can improve soil structure, enhance moisture retention, and provide a steady supply of nutrients to your plants. Mulching with organic materials like straw or leaves is another effective practice that helps conserve moisture, suppress weeds, and, over time, break down into compost, further enriching the soil.

Incorporating these practices into your gardening routine not only boosts your garden's productivity but also its sustainability. By fostering a healthy soil environment through nitrogen-fixing plants, crop rotation, composting, and mulching, you create a garden that is a source of great joy and produce and a vibrant ecosystem that supports and sustains a diverse array of life.

3.3 Pest Repelling Plant Pairings That Work

When you think about keeping your garden healthy, managing pests is undoubtedly at the forefront of your considerations. Chemical pesticides, while effective, often come with unwanted side effects, like harming beneficial insects and contributing to chemical runoffs that can negatively impact the environment. This is where the magic of using specific, natural plant pairings can make a significant difference. Not only do these pairings reduce the reliance on chemicals, but they also promote a balanced ecosystem where plants help each other fend off pests naturally.

Natural Repellents

Certain plants are gifted with natural abilities to repel various garden pests due to their specific chemical properties. For example, when planted near roses, garlic can help repel aphids that often plague these flowers. The sulfur compounds naturally produced by garlic serve as an effective deterrent against these pests. Similarly, chrysanthemums contain pyrethrin, a natural insecticide that repels roaches, beetles, ticks, and silverfish, making them excellent companions for various vegetable and flower plants. Integrating these natural repellents into your garden keeps pests at bay and adds variety and beauty to your plant layout. Strategically placing these plants around the perimeter of your garden or interspersing them among your crops can create a barrier that protects your entire garden from common pests.

Targeted Combinations

To tailor your pest management strategy, consider combinations that target specific pests. For instance, planting nasturtiums near your squash plants can help deter squash bugs, a common pest that can be hard to manage once they establish themselves. Nasturtiums act as a trap crop, attracting pests away from the main crop. Similarly, radishes can draw leafminers away from spinach. The leafminers prefer radish leaves, sparing your spinach from damage. These targeted strategies help manage pests and allow you to do so without harming the beneficial insects contributing to pollination and overall garden health.

Herbal Guardians

Using aromatic herbs is another effective way to manage pests in the garden. Herbs like rosemary and thyme produce strong scents that naturally repel many insects and can protect neighbouring plants. For example, planting rosemary near beans can help keep bean beetles away, while thyme can deter cabbage worms when planted near cabbages. Moreover, these herbs are not just functional; they are culinary delights, adding value to your garden in beauty and utility. Their strong odours mask the scent of your vegetables, making it harder for pests to locate their target plants.

Companion Planting as IPM

Integrating these pest-repelling plants into your garden aligns with Integrated Pest Management (IPM) principles. This broader strategy combines biological, cultural, physical, and chemical tools to manage pests in an environmentally and economically sound manner. Companion planting plays a crucial role in this approach by using biological means to manage pests. It reduces the need for chemical interventions, promotes biodiversity, and enhances crop and garden health. This method supports a sustainable gardening practice and fosters a holistic approach to garden management, focusing on preventing pest problems before they become severe.

By adopting these companion planting strategies, you actively contribute to a healthier, more sustainable garden ecosystem. You encourage natural processes that keep pests in check and enhance your garden's overall resilience and productivity. This approach makes gardening more enjoyable and rewarding as you watch your plants thrive together, supporting each other in more ways than one.

3.4 Companion Flowers: More Than Just Pretty Faces

When you think of flowers in a garden, your mind might first paint a picture of beauty and splendour, bursts of colours that catch the eye and ignite the senses. However, flowers aren't just about adding aesthetic value; they play multifaceted roles in your garden's ecosystem. From attracting vital pollinators to providing edible and medicinal benefits and even serving as natural pest deterrents, flowers have a profound impact on the health and productivity of your garden space. Let's explore how integrating certain flowers can bring these benefits, transforming your garden into a functional showcase of nature's wonder.

Pollinators like bees, butterflies, and hummingbirds are essential for pollinating many crops, and flowers are the perfect lure for these helpful creatures. Plants such as lavender, salvia, and cosmos are visually appealing and highly effective at attracting many pollinators. Lavender, with its soothing fragrance and rich nectar, is particularly good at attracting bees, among the most important pollinators in most gardens. Similarly, the bright and open blooms of the cosmos provide an easy landing pad for butterflies. Planting these alongside your vegetable plots or fruit trees can significantly enhance pollination, yielding better crops. Additionally, the presence of diverse pollinators helps maintain the balance of the ecosystem in your garden, ensuring that plants reproduce and thrive.

Beyond their beauty and role in attracting pollinators, many flowers also offer edible and medicinal properties that can be a delightful addition to your home remedies and culinary experiments. Consider calendula and nasturtiums; both are not only beautiful, but their flowers are edible. Calendula is known for its therapeutic properties in healing salves and creams due to its anti-inflammatory and antibacterial qualities. With their peppery flavour, Nasturtiums can be a colourful and spicy addition to salads. Moreover, the versatility of these plants extends beyond the plate; they are also used in companion planting to enhance the growth and flavour of various vegetables and deter pests with their strong scents and vibrant colours that act as decoys.

Flowers also benefit the garden by serving as natural pest deterrents, reducing the need for chemical pesticides. Marigolds are a prime example; their bright blooms are cheerful and release a scent that repels pests like nematodes and tomato hornworms. Additionally, the sticky sap of marigolds can trap more minor pests, preventing them from damaging more vulnerable plants. Sunflowers, towering and stately, can draw aphids away from more sensitive plants, acting as a sacrificial crop that keeps pests occupied while other plants grow unhindered. Integrating these flowers into your garden adds layers of colours and textures and fortifies your garden's defences against common pests, enhancing overall plant health.

Incorporating flowers into your garden design considers their aesthetic appeal and role in the ecosystem. Designing with flowers can be as strategic as artistic, ensuring that every plant fulfils multiple roles. For instance, a border of lavender along a vegetable garden not only adds a splash of colour and fragrance but also enhances biodiversity, attracting and sustaining a variety of pollinators and beneficial insects. Similarly, interspersing garlic chives and chamomile among vegetables can improve soil health and deter pests, all while adding beauty and variety to your garden landscape. This approach to using flowers marries functionality with visual appeal, creating a dynamic, interactive, and sensory-rich garden.

By embracing the multifunctional nature of flowers, you enrich your garden visually and ecologically. Flowers can transform a garden from a mere collection of plants into a vibrant, thriving ecosystem where beauty and utility are intrinsically intertwined. As you plan your garden, consider flowers not just as ornamental additions but as essential partners that contribute to the health, productivity, and sustainability of your gardening efforts. This holistic approach enhances the enjoyment and satisfaction of gardening and promotes a deeper connection with the natural world, fostering a garden that is genuinely in tune with the environment.

3.5 Maximizing Small Spaces with Strategic Pairings

When working with limited space, every inch counts, and knowing how to pair plants strategically can turn even the most minor patch into a prolific garden. Intensive planting techniques are your best friends here, focusing on maximizing productivity by carefully selecting and positioning plants to take full advantage of every square inch. A practical method is square foot gardening, where the garden space is divided into small square sections, typically 1x1 foot each. This method allows you to easily manage different crops in a defined area, ensuring that each plant has enough space to thrive without wasting any precious soil. For example, you might plant one tomato per square foot, but you can fit up to sixteen radishes in the same space. This method not only optimizes the use of space but also helps manage crop rotation and track plant growth.

Regarding container gardening, the key is choosing suitable companions that can coexist comfortably without competing too aggressively for nutrients and water. A classic pairing is tomatoes and basil in a large pot, where the basil helps repel pests naturally and can benefit from the partial shade provided by the tomato plant's foliage when the sun is at its peak. Another brilliant pairing is strawberries and chives; the chives help fend off strawberry pests and diseases, and their slim profile doesn't compete with the spreading habit of the strawberries. Containers offer the flexibility to move plants around, which is handy if you need to adjust their sun exposure or protect them from harsh weather conditions.

Vertical gardens are an excellent solution for those who want to grow more in less space. Utilizing vertical space increases your planting area and adds aesthetics to your garden. When planning a vertical garden, consider how plants can benefit each other. For instance, planting vining beans at the base of a trellis with cucumbers can allow both plants to climb up, maximizing their sun exposure and air circulation, which are crucial for healthy growth and fruit production. This setup saves ground space, makes harvesting more accessible, and helps keep pests at bay, as the airflow reduces mildew and fungal infections.

Interplanting is another technique that can significantly increase the yield of your small garden. This involves planting different crops that have complementary growth cycles and nutritional needs. For example, sowing fast-growing spinach between rows of slower-growing broccoli can maximize space usage; the spinach will be ready to harvest by the time the broccoli begins to mature. Additionally, interplanting flowers like marigolds or nasturtiums can help improve biodiversity, attract pollinators, and naturally repel pests, enhancing your garden's overall health and yield. This method not only optimizes space but also creates a living mosaic of plants, each contributing to the health and beauty of the garden.

Implementing these strategies allows you to transform any small space into a productive and beautiful garden oasis. Whether working with a few containers on a balcony or a small backyard plot, understanding how to pair plants strategically allows you to harness the full potential of your gardening space, ensuring that no area is underutilized. The joy of harvesting various crops from such a compact space is rewarding and a testament to the creativity and efficiency that companion planting offers.

3.6 Unusual and Exotic Companion Plant Pairings

Exploring the realm of companion planting often brings to mind common pairings like tomatoes and basil or carrots and onions. However, stepping beyond these familiar duos opens up a world of intriguing and less typical combinations that can invigorate your garden with unique benefits and exotic flair. Embracing less common plants and pairings diversifies your garden's ecosystem and enhances its resilience and productivity through novel interactions and mutual support.

Beyond the Basics

Using unusual and exotic plants in companion planting can introduce a range of unique benefits. For instance, consider the inclusion of caper bushes in your Mediterranean garden settings. Capers, with their deep root systems, can help break up compact soils, making them more accessible for the shallower roots of neighbouring herbs like rosemary or lavender. Another fascinating plant to consider is the toothache plant (Spilanthus acmella), which, when planted alongside your herbs, can deter pests with its high pyrethrin content, a natural insecticide. These plants add a unique visual element to your garden and contribute functional advantages that are less commonly exploited in typical garden settings.

Tropical and Temperate Mixes

Mixing tropical and temperate plants in the same garden can seem challenging due to their differing climate needs. However, with thoughtful planning and placement, you can create microclimates within your garden that cater to both types. For example, planting banana plants can provide much-needed shade and humidity for heat-sensitive plants like ferns. This helps the ferns thrive without direct sunlight and utilizes the vertical space and the tropical appearance of the banana plants to create a lush, layered garden effect. Additionally, the large leaves of the banana plants reduce water evaporation from the soil, benefiting the entire planting area.

Another strategy is to use tropical plants as seasonal companions in temperate zones. Plants like cannas or elephant ears can be planted during the warmer months to provide shade and moisture retention for companions such as lettuce or spinach, which might otherwise struggle with the summer heat. When the cooler weather arrives, these tropical plants can be replaced or moved indoors, while the temperate plants flourish in more openly sunny spots.

Aromatic Combinations

The role of scent in the garden extends beyond just pleasing the gardener's nose. Aromatic plants can be powerful allies in managing pests and enhancing the growth of companions. For example, the intense fragrance of certain exotic herbs, such as lemon verbena or eucalyptus, can mask the scent of nearby vegetables, making it harder for pests to locate their target. These strong scents can also attract beneficial insects that prey on common garden pests. Integrating these aromatic plants into your garden provides pest management benefits and offers fresh aromas and flavours for your kitchen.

Moreover, some exotic aromatic plants can have allelopathic properties, meaning they release chemicals that can inhibit the growth of certain weeds or pests. Tagetes minuta, often known as Mexican marigold, has roots that secrete a substance which deters nematodes and even some invasive weeds. Planting Mexican marigolds near your vegetable beds can help control soil-borne pests and reduce your need for manual weeding or chemical herbicides.

Experimental Pairings

Embracing the experimental spirit in gardening can lead to discovering new plant interactions and benefits. While traditional pairings provide a tried and tested foundation, experimenting with unconventional plant combinations can yield surprising and beneficial results. For instance, pairing vanilla orchids with citrus trees in a greenhouse setting allows the orchid to climb and benefit from the humid environment, which benefits both plants. Similarly, integrating aquatic plants like watercress into a hydroponic system with leafy greens can improve water quality and provide nutrients, enhancing overall plant health and yield.

When experimenting with new pairings, monitoring the plants closely for signs of success or stress is essential. Keep a garden journal to record observations and adjustments, noting everything from growth patterns to pest activity. This helps refine your companion planting strategies and contributes to a broader understanding of plant interactions, which can be shared with the gardening community.

Expanding your garden's diversity with these unusual and experimental pairings enhances its beauty and productivity and turns it into a vibrant laboratory for ecological exploration. This approach encourages a deeper engagement with your garden, where each planting season becomes an opportunity for discovery and innovation.

As this chapter wraps up, we've traversed from traditional companion planting concepts into the exciting territory of unusual and exotic pairings. Each plant interaction we've explored offers unique benefits and challenges, paving the way for a garden that's not only productive but also a reflection of ecological creativity and stewardship. The next chapter will explore implementing these concepts into your garden, focusing on practical steps and strategies to transform your companion planting plans into lush, thriving realities.

FOUR

Implementing Companion Planting in Your Garden

Stepping into your garden, you roll up your sleeves, ready to transform this patch of earth into a thriving ecosystem where plants grow and support one another. The excitement of starting can feel like setting the stage for a grand performance where each plant plays a crucial role. Let's dive into the very foundation of this performance: preparing the soil. As a firm foundation supports a house, well-prepared soil supports your garden. Whether you're a seasoned green thumb or just starting your gardening adventure, understanding how to prepare your soil correctly will set you up for success.

4.1 Preparing the Soil for Companion Planting

Soil Testing

Before you plant a single seed, knowing the starting point of your soil's health is essential. Soil testing is a critical first step as it reveals your soil's nutrient levels and pH balance, significantly influencing plant health and growth. Think of it as a medical check-up for your garden. By understanding your soil's current condition, you can make informed decisions about what amendments it might need. This could be lime to adjust the pH or specific nutrients lacking. Most local cooperative extensions offer soil testing services, or you can purchase a home testing kit. Once you have your results, you'll have a clearer picture of what your soil is already good at providing and what you might need to add to create the perfect environment for your companion plants.

Organic Matter Addition

Adding organic matter is one of the best things you can do for your soil. This can include things like compost, decayed leaves, or well-rotted manure. Why is organic matter so beneficial? It improves soil structure, which helps with both water retention and drainage. Plus, it provides essential nutrients as it decomposes, which supports ongoing plant health. When incorporating organic matter, spread it evenly over your garden bed and work it into the soil. This feeds your soil and makes it easier for plant roots to penetrate deep into the ground, accessing nutrients and moisture. It's like giving your plants a built-in buffet of everything they crave right where they need it the most.

Natural Fertilizers

While organic matter provides some nutrients, your soil needs more help, especially with sandy soil or heavy clay. This is where natural fertilizers come into play. Unlike synthetic fertilizers, natural fertilizers release nutrients slowly, reducing the risk of over-fertilization and providing a steady supply of nutrients to your plants. They also don't disturb the beneficial microorganisms and worms in your soil, which are crucial for maintaining soil health. Options like bone meal for phosphorus, blood meal for nitrogen, and green sand for potassium are all practical choices. When applied according to your soil test recommendations, these natural fertilizers can significantly boost the growth and health of your companion plants without the harsh effects of synthetic alternatives.

Soil Aeration and Drainage

Finally, let's talk about aeration and drainage—two factors that might not seem thrilling but are vital to plant health. Compacted soil can make it difficult for roots to grow and limit the air and water that gets to them. On the other hand, soil that drains too quickly might not retain enough water to support plant growth. To improve aeration and drainage, start by loosening the soil with a fork or tiller, being careful not to go too deep and disturb the natural soil structure. Consider adding coarse sand or gypsum to improve drainage if you have heavy clay soil. For sandy soil, more organic matter can help retain water and nutrients.

By taking the time to understand and prepare your soil correctly, you set the stage for a garden that is more than just a collection of plants. It becomes a dynamic ecosystem where each plant grows and supports its neighbours, creating a harmonious and productive garden. Remember, the healthier your soil and plants are, the more robust your entire garden ecosystem will be. So, let's give your garden the best possible start with soil ready to support a vibrant and thriving companion planting adventure.

4.2 Seed Starting and Transplanting Tips

When you're eager to see those little green shoots sprouting in your garden, starting from seed can be incredibly rewarding. It allows you a more comprehensive selection of plant varieties and gives you control over the growing process from the very start. Let's dive into some practical techniques to ensure your seedlings get the best possible start, preparing them to thrive alongside their companions in the garden.

Germination Techniques

Germinating seeds is much like baking a perfect loaf of bread; it requires attention to the right conditions—temperature and moisture being paramount. Most seeds germinate best in warm conditions, around 65-75°F. However, some specific types, like spinach or peas, might prefer cooler temperatures. Using a heat mat can help maintain consistent soil temperature, especially during cooler months or in colder climates. Moisture control is equally critical. Seeds need to be consistently moist but not soggy. Using a spray bottle to mist your seeds can keep them adequately hydrated without the risk of overwatering, which can lead to fungal diseases such as damping off. Covering your pots or trays with plastic wrap or a dome can help retain moisture and warmth, creating a mini greenhouse effect. Remove the cover once you see the first sprouts to prevent excess humidity, which can also encourage mould growth.

Potting Mixes

Choosing the right potting mix is crucial for the healthy growth of your seedlings. A good seed starting mix should be light and fluffy, allowing for excellent air circulation and proper drainage, essential for young roots to develop. Avoid using garden soil as it can be too heavy and may contain pathogens that could harm delicate seedlings. Look for mixes labelled explicitly for seed starting, or make your own by combining peat moss or coconut coir with perlite and vermiculite. This combination provides a sterile, nutrient-rich environment supporting the initial growth phase. Remember, the potting mix quality can significantly influence your plants' health and ability to withstand the transition to outdoor conditions.

Hardening Off

Once your seedlings have grown strong enough indoors, they must gradually acclimate to outdoor conditions, a process known as hardening off. This step is vital to prevent shock, which can stunt growth or kill young plants. Begin about a week before you plan to transplant them outside. Place your seedlings outdoors in a sheltered, partially shaded area for a few hours each day, gradually increasing their exposure to sun and wind. Be mindful of temperature changes; bring them back indoors if there's a frost risk or the weather turns harsh. This gradual introduction helps strengthen the plant's cell structure and reduces transplant shock, giving it a better chance to thrive once fully moved to your garden.

Transplant Timing and Technique

Timing is everything when it comes to transplanting. After developing their second set of true leaves, most seedlings are ready to move to the garden. This indicates that they are likely strong enough to endure the transplant process. When transplanting, it's essential to handle the delicate seedlings gently. Avoid grabbing them by the stems or leaves; instead, ease them out of their containers by pushing from the bottom or using a small tool to lift the root ball. If the roots are densely packed, gently tease them apart to encourage them to spread out in their new environment. Plant them at the same depth they were growing in their containers unless it's tomatoes, which can benefit from planting deeper to encourage more root growth along the buried stem.

When placing your seedlings in the garden, consider their future growth. Space them according to their mature size to ensure they have room to expand without overcrowding. Water them well after transplanting to help settle the soil around the roots and eliminate air pockets. A gentle watering with a seaweed extract or light fish emulsion solution can provide a nutrient boost and help reduce transplant stress. This attention to detail during transplanting helps your seedlings transition smoothly from their starter containers to becoming robust, productive plants in your companion garden.

By following these seed-starting and transplanting tips, you equip yourself with the knowledge to manage one of the most exciting phases of gardening. Watching the seeds you planted sprout, grow, and flourish is gratifying and a testament to your care and dedication to nurturing your garden from the ground up.

An e-meter can be a helpful way to monitor moisture levels, ensuring that you're providing just the right amount of water to keep all your companion plants healthy and thriving.

By mastering these watering techniques, you equip yourself with the knowledge to manage one of the most crucial aspects of gardening effectively. Whether choosing the right irrigation system, setting a thoughtful watering schedule, applying mulch to conserve moisture, or recognizing signs of water stress in your plants, each step contributes to a healthier garden. Remember, the goal is not just to water your plants but to nurture them in a way that promotes their best growth and productivity. With these strategies in hand, you're well on your way to becoming a gardener and a guardian of your thriving companion-planted garden.

4.3 Natural Solutions to Common Pest Problems

Tackling pests in your garden can often feel like a game of whack-a-mole; another appears when you think you've got them under control. However, by integrating natural pest management strategies into your companion planting, you can create a garden that is not only beautiful and productive but also maintains ecological balance. Let's explore some effective, environmentally friendly methods to keep pests at bay, enhancing the health and yield of your companion plants without resorting to harsh chemicals.

Biological Controls

Inviting beneficial insects into your garden is like hiring a team of tiny gardeners who work tirelessly to keep pest populations in check. These natural predators can dramatically reduce your need for other forms of pest control. Ladybugs, for instance, are voracious eaters of aphids, mites, and scale insects—all of which can be detrimental to your garden. Similarly, lacewings can be introduced to handle outbreaks of aphids and other soft-bodied pests. You can attract these beneficial insects by planting flowers they love, such as dill, fennel, and yarrow, or by purchasing them from a reputable garden supply store to release directly into your garden.

Another powerful ally in the biological control arsenal is the nematode, a microscopic worm that preys on soil-dwelling pests like cutworms and beetle larvae. Nematodes are applied as a soil drench, infiltrating the soil and reducing pest populations without harming your plants. It's a subtle yet highly effective way to protect your garden from the ground up. These methods not only keep harmful pests at bay but also support the biodiversity of your garden, making it a healthier environment for both plants and pollinators.

Physical Barriers

Sometimes, the best way to deal with pests is to keep them out entirely. Physical barriers like row covers or plant collars can protect young plants from insects and animals. Row covers, made of lightweight, translucent fabric, can be draped over plants to protect them from flying insects and birds while letting in sunlight and rain. These covers can be beneficial during the early stages of plant growth when they are most vulnerable. For plants at risk of soil-borne pests like cutworms, plant collars made from cardboard or plastic can be placed around the stem at soil level to deter these pests.

Another simple yet effective physical barrier is the use of garden netting. This can be draped over fruit bushes or young seedlings to protect them from birds and larger insects. The key is to ensure the netting is secured well and checked regularly to prevent any creatures from becoming trapped. By using these barriers, you protect your plants without chemical interventions, preserving the natural balance of your garden ecosystem.

Organic Pesticides

While the goal is to use them sparingly, there are times when organic pesticides can be helpful as a last resort. These products are derived from natural sources and are generally less environmentally harmful than synthetic pesticides. For instance, neem oil, derived from the seeds of the neem tree, is effective against a wide range of pests, including aphids, mites, and whiteflies. It works by disrupting the life cycle of pests, making it a potent addition to your pest control toolkit. Another option is insecticidal soap, which can tackle outbreaks of soft-bodied insects like aphids and spider mites.

When using organic pesticides, it's crucial to apply them correctly and at the right time—preferably in the evening or early morning to avoid harming beneficial insects like bees. Always follow the manufacturer's instructions to ensure you use the product safely and effectively. Remember, these treatments should be part of a broader pest management strategy that includes cultural and physical methods, ensuring your garden remains a healthy and thriving ecosystem.

Companion Plants as Repellents

One of the most delightful aspects of companion planting is the natural repellent properties that certain plants can offer. Many herbs, for instance, are not just for cooking; they also play a role in repelling unwanted insects. Basil emits a scent that repels flies and mosquitoes, making it a great companion for patio plantings or garden areas where you spend a lot of time. Similarly, chives can deter Japanese beetles and carrot flies, and their subtle onion scent is unnoticeable to humans once they bloom.

Another star in the pest repellent lineup is lavender. Known for its soothing aroma and beautiful purple flowers, lavender can repel moths, fleas, and flies. Planting it around seating areas or near doors can help reduce the presence of these pests in your outdoor living spaces. Additionally, the strong scent of garlic can deter deer and rabbits, two common garden nuisances. Planting garlic around the perimeter of your garden or near particularly vulnerable crops can help keep these critters at bay without the need for harsh repellents or fences.

Incorporating these natural solutions into your garden management strategy creates a more resilient and self-regulating garden. This reduces your reliance on chemical interventions and enhances your garden's overall health and productivity. Remember, the goal is to create a balance where plants can thrive with minimal interference, supported by the natural environment and its beneficial creatures.

4.4 Watering Techniques for Companion Planted Gardens

When nurturing a companion planted garden, understanding the art of watering isn't just about keeping your plants alive; it's about making them thrive. Each type of plant in your companion setup has unique watering needs; balancing these is a juggling act. However, with the proper techniques and tools, you can ensure that each plant receives just the right amount of moisture to flourish. Let's explore some effective irrigation systems and strategies to help you manage this vital aspect of gardening.

Irrigation systems can be a game-changer, especially in a diverse garden where plants with varying water needs live side by side. Drip irrigation systems are fantastic for delivering water directly to the base of each plant, minimizing waste and preventing the spread of leaf diseases that can occur with overhead watering. This system consists of a network of tubes that release water slowly at the root zone, where it's most needed. This targeted approach is water-efficient and ensures that each plant gets the right amount of hydration according to its specific needs. Soaker hoses, another excellent option, operate on a similar principle. These hoses are laid out along the ground and allow water to seep through their porous material, providing a steady, gentle water supply directly to the soil. The advantage of soaker hoses is their simplicity and ease of installation, making them ideal for garden beds and borders.

Choosing between these systems often depends on the layout and size of your garden and your budget. Drip systems can be more precise and customizable but may require more significant initial investment and some setup time. On the other hand, soaker hoses are generally more affordable and accessible to install, though they might not provide the same level of precision. Both systems are excellent choices for companion planting, as they allow you to tailor watering to the needs of different plants, promoting health and vigour in your diverse garden.

Watering Schedule

Determining a watering schedule that meets the needs of your companion plants is crucial. This schedule will vary depending on plant species, soil type, and weather conditions. Generally, it's best to water deeply and less frequently, encouraging plants to develop deep root systems, making them more drought-resistant and robust. Observe your plants and soil in the early morning to establish a schedule. If the soil feels dry an inch below the surface, it's usually a good sign that watering is needed. Additionally, consider the specific water needs of your plants: leafy vegetables and moisture-loving flowers may require more frequent watering than drought-tolerant herbs and succulents.

Creating a zone-based watering system within your garden can help manage different watering needs efficiently. You can control the water each zone receives by grouping plants with similar moisture requirements and using valves or hose splitters. This method ensures that each plant community gets just the right amount of water without over- or under-watering, which can lead to stress and disease.

Mulching for Moisture

Mulching is another essential technique in effective water management. Applying a layer of organic material like straw, wood chips, or leaf mould around your plants can significantly reduce soil evaporation. Mulch acts as an insulating layer, keeping the soil cool and moist even during hot days. It also helps prevent weed growth, which can compete with your plants for water. When applying mulch, leave some space around the base of each plant to avoid moisture buildup, which could cause rot or fungal diseases. The thickness of the mulch layer can vary, but a general rule of thumb is to maintain a layer about 2-3 inches thick. This is usually sufficient to conserve moisture while allowing rain and irrigation water to penetrate the soil.

Signs of Overwatering and Underwatering

Recognizing the signs of overwatering and underwatering can save your plants from stress and disease. Overwatered plants often exhibit symptoms such as yellowing leaves, soft and mushy stems or roots, and a general lack of vigour. This is usually due to oxygen-deprived roots, which can lead to root rot. On the other hand, underwatered plants typically show signs like wilting, dry and brittle leaves, and stunted growth. Monitoring soil moisture regularly and adjusting your watering habits accordingly is essential to avoid these issues. Using a simple soil moisturizer, you choose organic or inorganic materials; the proper application and maintenance of mulch can profoundly affect your garden's health and productivity, making it a lusher, more vibrant space for all your companion plants to thrive.

4.5 Mulching: Types and Techniques for Companion Planting

Mulching is like giving your garden a cosy blanket, one that not only keeps it warm but also nurtures its overall health. When delving into companion planting, mulching can play multiple roles, from conserving moisture to suppressing weeds and enhancing your garden's visual appeal. Understanding the various types of mulch and their specific benefits can help you make informed choices that will bolster the health and productivity of your companion plants.

Let's explore the different types of mulch you can use in your garden. Organic mulches, such as straw, bark chips, and leaf mould, are popular because they decompose over time, adding valuable organic matter back into the soil. Straw is particularly great for vegetable gardens; it's light, easy to spread, and breaks down fairly quickly, which enriches the soil with nutrients. Bark chips, on the other hand, decompose slower and are ideal for pathways or around perennial plants where you don't disturb the soil often. Leaf mould, made from decomposed leaves, is a fantastic mulch for improving soil structure and is particularly beneficial in sandy or clay soils. For those looking for longer-lasting options, inorganic mulches like stones or landscape fabric can be used. These materials don't improve soil structure or fertility. Still, they are excellent for controlling weeds and retaining soil moisture in decorative areas or around established plants where little soil amendment is needed.

Applying mulch correctly is crucial to avoid problems such as rot or unwanted pest habitats. When mulching around companion plants, ensure that the mulch does not come into direct contact with the stems or leaves. This practice helps prevent moisture-related diseases and stem rot. The ideal method is to lay mulch around the base of each plant, extending out to the drip line—the area directly below the outer circumference of the plant's branches. This ensures the roots are covered and protected, which helps with water retention and temperature regulation. Be careful not to bury smaller plants or disrupt their growth using heavier mulches like bark chips. A layer of 2-3 inches of mulch is typically sufficient to suppress weeds and retain moisture without suffocating the plant roots.

The benefits of mulching extend beyond just beautification. By covering the soil, mulch helps maintain a more consistent soil temperature, protecting plant roots from extreme heat in summer and insulating them from cold in the winter. This temperature control is particularly beneficial in companion planting setups where plants of varying hardiness may be grown together. Mulch also helps retain moisture in the soil by reducing surface evaporation, which is crucial during hot or dry periods. This can lead to more efficient water use and make your gardening efforts more sustainable. Additionally, as organic mulches decompose, they provide a steady supply of nutrients to the soil, reducing the need for chemical fertilizers and enhancing the growth and health of your companion plants.

Refreshing and replacing mulch at the right time is critical to maintaining its benefits. Organic mulches must be refreshed yearly as they break into the soil. This ensures your garden continues to reap the benefits of fresh organic matter and maintains its aesthetic appeal. The best time to refresh mulch is in late spring after the soil has warmed up. This helps keep the soil warm and moist throughout the growing season. If you notice that the mulch is matting or forming a crust, it's a good sign that it must be fluffed or replaced to allow water and air to continue penetrating the soil effectively. For inorganic mulches, periodic checking for displacement and thinning areas is necessary to ensure adequate coverage and effectiveness.

By incorporating these mulching techniques into your companion planting strategy, you not only enhance the growth conditions for your plants but also contribute to a more sustainable and visually appealing garden environment.

4.6 Seasonal Care and Maintenance of Companion Plants

As the seasons change, so do your garden's needs. Adapting your care strategies to accommodate these shifts is crucial for maintaining a vibrant and productive companion planting setup. Each season brings specific tasks that help prepare your plants for the upcoming weather changes, ensuring they continue to thrive and support one another.

Spring Preparation

Spring is a time of renewal in the garden, and getting your companion plants ready for this growth period is critical. Start by clearing away any debris or old mulch from the previous season, as these can harbour pests and diseases over the winter. It's also an excellent time to add a fresh layer of compost around your plants. This feeds the soil and introduces beneficial microbes that help keep the soil healthy and nutrient-rich.

Pruning is another vital spring task. Pruning helps remove dead or damaged branches for perennial plants, encouraging new growth and more robust plants. Use sharp, clean pruning tools to make clean cuts that heal quickly. Proper pruning can enhance the display of blooms and maintain the desired shape of certain flowering plants, such as roses or peonies.

Fertilizing in spring is also crucial, especially for nutrient-hungry plants that are starting to grow again. Use a balanced, slow-release organic fertilizer to provide a steady supply of nutrients throughout the growing season. This fertilizer minimizes the risk of nutrient runoff and ensures that your plants get the nutrition they need without overwhelming them all at once.

Summer Upkeep

Regular maintenance is essential to keep your garden healthy during the warm summer. Regular checks for pests and diseases can help catch any issues before they become serious problems. Look for signs of infestation or illness, such as discoloured leaves, stunted growth, or unusual spots. Early detection and natural interventions, like removing affected parts or applying organic treatments, can often prevent the spread and save your plants.

Water stress is another common issue in summer, especially during hot, dry periods. Watch your plants for signs of water stress, including wilting or yellowing leaves. Adjust your watering schedule as needed to ensure all plants receive adequate moisture. Remember, overwatering can be as harmful as underwatering, so it's essential to strike the right balance based on each plant's needs.

Fall Activities

Preparing your garden for winter is the next step as the growing season winds down. Applying a thick layer of mulch around your plants can help protect their roots from freezing temperatures and retain soil moisture during the cold months. Choose an organic mulch, such as straw or shredded leaves, which will continue to enrich the soil as it decomposes over the winter.

Cover crops like clover or winter rye are another effective way to enhance soil health during the winter. These crops help prevent soil erosion, add organic matter, and fix nitrogen in the soil, which benefits the next season's plants. Once spring arrives, simply till these cover crops into the soil to add nutrients and improve soil structure before planting your main crops.

Winter Care

Winter care is about the protection and preservation of perennial companion plants. In colder climates, frost can damage sensitive plants. Applying frost covers or burlap wraps can provide extra insulation against harsh temperatures. For particularly delicate perennials, consider moving them to a sheltered location, such as a greenhouse or indoors, where they can be kept safe until spring.

Regular checks during the winter months are also necessary. Ensure your protective measures guard against the weather, and adjust as required. This might include reinforcing mulch or adding additional coverings during freezing spells.

As this chapter closes, we've covered essential seasonal care techniques that ensure your companion plants are well-prepared for each part of the year. These practices form the backbone of a resilient and flourishing garden, from spring rejuvenation and summer vigilance to fall preparation and winter protection. The next chapter will focus on advanced companion planting strategies, where we'll delve deeper into optimizing your garden's potential through innovative planting techniques and long-term planning strategies. This ongoing journey of learning and adaptation enhances your immediate gardening success and contributes to a sustainable and bio-diverse garden ecosystem that thrives year after year.

Make a Difference with Your Review

Companion Planting for Beginners
Creating Eco-Friendly Gardens for Sustainable, Healthier Plants: Foster Biodiversity and Minimize Chemicals - Tackle Pest Problems Naturally

Did you know that sharing your thoughts can help others grow? Let's make a difference together!

Would you help someone you've never met, even if you didn't get credit for it?

This person is just like you—curious about gardening but unsure where to start. Our mission is to make **companion planting** easy and fun for everyone.

This is where you come in. Many people choose books based on reviews. So, I'm asking you to help a fellow gardener by leaving a review of this book.

Your review takes less than a minute but can mean the world to someone starting their garden. It could help

- ...one more person begins their gardening journey.
- ...one more family grow their own food.
- ...one more reader discovers the joy of plants working together.

To feel great about helping others, all you need to do is leave a review. Just scan the QR code below to share your thoughts:

Thank you from the bottom of my heart. Now, let's get back to our gardening adventure!

Your biggest fan, Terra Verde Writers.

FIVE

Advanced Companion Planting Strategies

Imagine your garden as a small but mighty ecosystem, where every element, from the tiniest herb to the tallest sunflower, plays a critical role in creating a sustainable, thriving space. This chapter dives into the fascinating world of permaculture—a philosophy that mimics the patterns and relationships found in nature. By applying permaculture principles to companion planting, you're not just growing plants but cultivating a self-sustaining environment that flourishes with minimal human intervention over time.

5.1 Creating a Permaculture Garden with Companion Planting

Permaculture Principles

At its heart, permaculture is about working with nature instead of against it. This approach hinges on three core tenets: care for the earth, care for the people, and fair share, which involves limiting consumption and redistributing surplus. In the context of a companion planting garden, these principles guide you to create systems that sustain themselves. For example, planting nitrogen-fixing legumes like peas and beans alongside nitrogen-hungry crops such as corn and squash optimizes space. It ensures that your garden remains fertile year after year without chemical fertilizers.

Permaculture also emphasizes the importance of observing and interacting with your garden. This means taking the time to understand your garden space's unique patterns and cycles, from sunlight and shadow movements to natural water flow. By tuning into these natural rhythms, you can design your garden layout to harness maximum efficiency and productivity without exerting unnecessary effort or resources.

Designing for Sustainability

Creating a garden that mimics natural ecosystems involves thoughtful design that goes beyond just plant selection. Start by mapping out your space, considering elements like wind, sun exposure, and natural slopes. Use this information to place plants where they will benefit most strategically. For instance, taller plants that require more sunlight can be placed in the sunniest part of your garden, while shorter, shade-tolerant plants can grow in their shadow. This maximises light exposure and protects more sensitive plants from too much sun.

Another aspect of sustainable design is creating zones based on the frequency of human use. Place high-maintenance or frequently harvested plants like herbs and salads close to your house, while more self-sufficient plants can reside further away. This zoning saves energy and makes your gardening tasks more efficient.

Integrating Animals

Animals play a pivotal role in a permaculture garden, contributing to the biodiversity and sustainability of the ecosystem. Chickens, for example, can be invaluable. They provide eggs and help with pest control by eating insects and weeds. Moreover, their scratching and foraging activities naturally aerate the soil, and their droppings provide a rich source of nutrients.

Bees are another crucial component. Setting up a hive in your garden enhances pollination, essential for fruit and seed production. The presence of bees also increases the yield and quality of crops, ensuring a more bountiful harvest. When integrating animals, always ensure their needs are met in a way that benefits them and the garden, creating a harmonious environment where all elements support each other.

Water Management

In permaculture, effective water management is crucial and involves more than just watering plants. It's about designing your garden to mimic the natural water cycle and make the most of the water you have. Techniques like rainwater harvesting and swales—shallow trenches dug along the contour of the land—can significantly improve water efficiency. Swales capture rainwater and allow it to slowly infiltrate the soil, recharging groundwater and providing moisture to plants long after rainfall.

Another innovative water management strategy is the creation of rain gardens. These are small depressions in the landscape designed to collect and filter runoff water from roofs, driveways, and other impervious surfaces. Planting water-loving plants in these areas utilises this runoff and helps filter pollutants, improving water quality before it seeps back into the ground or enters the water system.

By embracing these advanced strategies, you transform your garden into a self-regulating ecosystem that produces abundant food and promotes a sustainable and environmentally friendly gardening practice. As you implement these concepts, remember that permaculture is not a one-size-fits-all solution but a flexible approach that adapts to your garden's unique conditions. Whether you're a seasoned gardener or just starting, integrating these principles can lead to more resilient, productive, and sustainable gardening practices.

5.2 Bio-Intensive Companion Planting Methods

Double-Digging for Soil Health

You'll want to embrace double-digging to give your garden a robust foundation. This labour-intensive but highly effective method involves digging down two spade depths in your garden beds and is particularly beneficial as you prepare for bio-intensive companion planting. What double-digging does is aerate the deeper layers of soil, which often go untouched in regular gardening practices. This aeration allows roots to penetrate more deeply, improves drainage, and enhances the soil's ability to retain nutrients.

First, remove the top layer of soil, setting it aside. Then, loosen the next layer without turning it over, which can help maintain the existing microbial structure. After that, return the first layer of soil mixed with well-decomposed compost or other organic matter. This enriches the soil and optimizes conditions for beneficial microbial activity that supports plant health. The result? You create a deeply nourished bed that encourages extensive root growth and water retention, setting the stage for a thriving garden that needs less watering and is more resilient to drought. Implementing this method in your garden requires muscle and commitment, but plant health and productivity payoff is well worth the effort.

Close Spacing of Plants

In bio-intensive gardening, close spacing of plants plays a pivotal role in creating a microclimate where plants can support each other's growth. This method reduces the space weeds have to grow, significantly decreasing the need for weeding. More importantly, when plants are spaced closely, they create a living mulch, shading the soil with their leaves, which keeps the soil moist and cool. This natural shade also slows the evaporation of water from the soil, meaning you'll need to water less frequently, conserving water while maintaining healthy soil moisture levels.

Moreover, close spacing can enhance the symbiotic relationships between different plants. For example, tall sunflowers can provide shade for heat-sensitive lettuce, while the lettuce can keep the soil cool and moist for the sunflowers, which prefer not to have their roots in hot soil. This strategy maximizes your garden space and fosters a supportive environment where plants help meet each other's needs, leading to a healthier, more productive garden.

Companion Planting Guilds

The concept of planting guilds is a cornerstone of bio-intensive companion planting. A guild is a group of plants synergistically supporting each other's growth and survival. Each guild member contributes differently—some attract beneficial insects, some repel pests, others fix nitrogen in the soil, and some might provide necessary shade or support. For instance, a classic guild might include corn, beans, and squash—often called the "Three Sisters." In this guild, the corn provides a natural trellis for the beans to climb, the beans fix nitrogen to benefit all three, and the sprawling squash shades the ground, helping to retain soil moisture and suppress weeds.

Creating influential guilds requires understanding different plants' roles and how their interactions benefit the group. When designing your guilds, consider factors like root depth, nutrient requirements, and growth patterns to ensure that plants do not compete but complement each other. For example, deep-rooted plants can be paired with shallow-rooted ones to optimize nutrient uptake from different soil levels without direct competition.

Crop Rotation in Bio-Intensive Planting

Crop rotation is an invaluable strategy within bio-intensive companion planting, helping to maintain soil health and reduce the buildup of pests and diseases. By rotating crops through different parts of the garden each year, you can avoid depleting the soil of specific nutrients that certain plants use in high amounts. For example, heavy feeders like tomatoes can be followed the next year by nitrogen-fixing legumes, which help to replenish the soil.

Advanced crop rotation involves rotating crops annually and planning several years to balance the soil's nutrient profile and structure. This long-term strategy helps break the life cycles of pests and diseases that thrive under continuous cropping conditions. It's also a thoughtful way to plan your planting schedule, ensuring that each garden section provides optimal conditions for the crops grown there based on previous and future plantings. This systematic approach enhances the sustainability of your gardening efforts and boosts your garden ecosystem's overall productivity and health.

By integrating these bio-intensive methods into your companion planting strategy, you are setting up a system that supports robust plant growth and promotes a sustainable, self-reliant garden. Whether through thorough soil preparation via double-digging, the strategic close spacing of plants, the thoughtful creation of planting guilds, or the meticulous planning of crop rotation, each technique offers a pathway to a more productive and environmentally friendly garden. As you implement these methods, you'll likely discover a deeper connection with your garden as a living ecosystem, where each element works harmoniously to create a much greater whole than the sum of its parts.

5.3 Companion Planting for Greenhouse Gardens

When you step into a greenhouse, you enter a world where the climate is yours to control. This enclosed space offers a unique opportunity to extend growing seasons and optimize plant health by carefully managing temperature, humidity, and airflow. Managing these elements effectively can turn your greenhouse into a year-round garden sanctuary, supporting a diverse range of companion plants that benefit one another.

Microclimate Management

Creating the ideal microclimate within your greenhouse begins with understanding the specific needs of your plants. Temperature control is crucial, as even a few degrees can significantly impact plant health and productivity. During the colder days;

Maintaining a consistent and adequate temperature protects plants from frost and encourages continued growth. This can be achieved through various heating solutions such as space heaters, heated propagation mats, or even utilizing the thermal mass of water barrels, which absorb heat during the day and release it at night. In contrast, the summer months require active cooling strategies such as shade cloths or ventilating fans to prevent overheating, which can be detrimental.

Humidity and airflow are equally important in a greenhouse setting. Too much moisture can lead to fungal diseases, while too little can stress plants and inhibit their growth. Striking the right balance often involves a combination of ventilation to bring in fresh air and exhaust excess moisture and humidity control techniques such as misting systems, which can help increase humidity levels when they dip too low. Proper airflow also ensures that temperature and humidity are evenly distributed throughout the space, preventing the formation of microclimates that could negatively affect plant health. Strategically placed fans or regularly opening vents can facilitate this airflow, ensuring each plant receives its ideal environmental conditions.

Season Extension

One of the most significant advantages of greenhouse gardening is extending the growing season of many plants. With a greenhouse, you're no longer strictly bound by the seasonal constraints of your climate zone. This means you can start seedlings earlier in the spring and keep producing well into the fall or even winter, depending on your setup. For companion planting, this can be particularly beneficial. For instance, tender herbs and greens, which might wilt under the harsh midsummer sun, can thrive alongside more heat-tolerant companions when grown in a controlled greenhouse environment.

Moreover, the extended season allows for greater flexibility in crop rotation and succession planting, critical components of effective companion planting. You could, for instance, follow a summer crop of tomatoes with a fall crop of greens, followed by overwintering garlic. Each plant in this sequence benefits its successor through pest suppression, soil improvement, or simply by making better use of the space and resources available throughout the year.

Pest Control in a Controlled Environment

While greenhouses provide some natural protection against pests by acting as a physical barrier, they are not impervious. The controlled environment of a greenhouse can sometimes exacerbate pest issues if not managed correctly. Integrated Pest Management (IPM) approaches are ideal in these settings. This might involve introducing beneficial insects that prey on harmful pests or implementing trap crops that attract pests away from your main crops. For example, planting marigolds can help control nematodes in the soil, while a small planting of aphid-attracting plants near the ventilation can lure these pests away from your main crops.

Regular monitoring is key to effective pest control in a greenhouse. By closely monitoring your plants and quickly addressing any signs of pests, you can prevent minor issues from becoming significant infestations. This proactive approach keeps your plants healthier and reduces the need for chemical interventions, which can disrupt the delicate balance of your companion planting system.

Maximizing Space

Utilizing every inch of space efficiently is particularly important in a greenhouse, where you have a finite area to work with. Vertical gardening and tiered planting structures can significantly increase your growing space. Climbing plants like peas and beans can be grown up trellises, freeing up ground space for shorter, shade-tolerant plants like spinach or lettuce. Similarly, tiered benches or shelves can house smaller pots of herbs or flowers, which can benefit from being closer to the light source.

Implementing these vertical and tiered planting strategies maximises space and promotes healthier plants by improving light exposure and air circulation. It allows you to create a diverse, multi-level garden ecosystem within your greenhouse, where each plant's placement is strategically chosen to benefit its neighbours by providing shade, improving air circulation, or simply making efficient use of available space.

5.4 Utilizing Vertical Space in Companion Planting

When you look at your garden, it's easy to see it as a flat canvas, but there's a whole dimension up there that's just brimming with potential! Vertical gardening isn't just a fantastic solution for those with limited space; it also adds an incredible layer of beauty and efficiency to any garden setup, especially when you integrate the principles of companion planting. Let's explore how you can elevate your gardening game by going vertical, focusing on structures, plant choices, and special care techniques that make the most of upward growth.

Vertical Structures

Introducing vertical structures such as trellises, towers, wall planters, and hanging baskets can dramatically transform the way you garden. These structures allow you to grow upwards, saving space and leading to healthier plants by improving air circulation and reducing susceptibility to pests. Trellises are perfect for climbing plants like beans and peas and vining flowers like morning glories. By pairing these climbers with lower-growing, shade-tolerant plants like spinach or lettuce, you can create a mutually beneficial arrangement—your climbers get the support they need to reach towards the sun, and in return, they provide some much-needed shade for those plants that thrive in cooler, less intense light conditions.

Another exciting vertical option is the use of wall planters or living walls. These can be used to grow herbs and smaller vegetables, such as strawberries or cherry tomatoes. When setting up a wall planter, consider companion planting herbs that naturally repel insects, thus providing a protective barrier for your entire garden. For example, planting basil alongside tomato plants enhances flavour and helps keep away flies and mosquitoes, which can be a nuisance during warm weather.

Plant Selection

Choosing the right plants for vertical growing involves considering their growth habits and requirements. Vining plants that climb naturally, like cucumbers, squash, and melons, are obvious choices for trellises. Vertical growth benefits these plants enormously, as it promotes better air circulation around the leaves, which helps to reduce the risk of fungal diseases. It also makes the fruit easier to harvest and less likely to suffer from soil-borne pests.

But climbers aren't the only plants that can benefit from vertical planting. Consider taller plants that can be staked, such as tomatoes and bell peppers. These plants can be paired with medium-height plants like basil or cilantro, which help to repel unwanted insects, and low-growing flowers such as marigolds, which can help deter soil pests and add a splash of colour to your vertical garden.

Watering and Maintenance

Watering in a vertical setting can be tricky, as gravity pulls water downwards, leading to uneven moisture distribution among your plants. Drip irrigation is an excellent solution for vertical gardens, as it delivers water directly to the base of each plant, ensuring that all plants receive an equal amount of water without wastage. This method also keeps the foliage dry, which is crucial in preventing the spread of diseases in densely planted areas.

Maintenance of your vertical garden also involves regular pruning and monitoring for pests. Pruning helps control the size and shape of your plants and encourages airflow and light penetration, which are essential for healthy growth. Keep an eye out for pests, especially aphids and spider mites, which can quickly colonize the undersides of leaves. Introducing natural predators like ladybugs or using organic insecticidal soaps can help manage these pests without resorting to harsh chemicals.

Maximizing Light Exposure

Proper light exposure is critical in a vertical garden. When arranging your plantings, place the taller and denser plants on the north side of your garden structure so they don't cast a shadow over shorter plants. Use the varying levels of sunlight exposure to your advantage by planting shade-loving plants beneath those that thrive in full sun. This strategic placement maximizes light efficiency and mirrors the layering found in natural ecosystems, where plants of different heights and types grow together symbiotically.

By incorporating these vertical gardening techniques, you can enhance the productivity and health of your garden and turn it into a stunning visual display. Whether you're crafting a lush wall of green, a towering trellis of blooms, or a functional and beautiful arrangement of tiers, vertical gardening opens up a whole new dimension in companion planting. Remember, the sky's the limit regarding your garden's potential!

5.5 Companion Planting and Hydroponic Systems

Hydroponic systems, where plants grow in a water-based, nutrient-rich solution without soil, offer a unique opportunity for gardeners to explore the dynamics of companion planting in a controlled environment. Embracing this method allows you to grow plants closer together, use water more efficiently, and increase yield and flavour profiles. However, not all plants are suited for this type of gardening, and knowing how to pair them effectively can make all the difference in your hydroponic adventure.

Let's identify which plants play well together in a hydroponic setup. Due to their similar nutrient needs and growth rates, leafy greens like lettuce, spinach, and Swiss chard are excellent choices. These can be effectively paired with herbs such as basil and cilantro, which have compatible nutrient demands and benefit from the slightly cooler microclimate the leafy greens help maintain in the system. This pairing reduces stress on each plant, leading to healthier, more robust growth. Additionally, the aromatic properties of herbs can help naturally deter pests, adding an extra layer of protection for your greens.

Tomatoes and peppers also make good companions in a hydroponic system because they thrive under similar light and temperature conditions. They can be trained upward when grown together, maximizing vertical space and improving air circulation around the plants. This can reduce certain fungal diseases that thrive in stagnant air conditions. Moreover, introducing marigolds into the mix can help manage pests naturally, as they repel nematodes and other pests that might otherwise thrive in the nutrient-rich hydroponic environment.

Managing nutrients in a hydroponic system can be quite the balancing act, especially when dealing with multiple types of plants. Each species has unique nutritional needs, and in a shared system, it's crucial to find a balance that meets all their needs without causing nutrient burn or deficiencies. Regular testing of water for pH and nutrient levels is essential. You might find that using a multi-part nutrient the solution, where each component can be adjusted independently, allows for greater control and customization based on the specific plants you are growing together.

For instance, leafy greens often require more nitrogen, whereas fruiting plants like tomatoes and peppers might need higher potassium and calcium levels as they mature. By adjusting the ratios of these nutrients in your system, you can cater to the needs of both types of plants without compromise. Additionally, implementing a recirculating system can help ensure that nutrients are evenly distributed, preventing buildup in certain system areas that could lead to root damage or nutrient imbalances.

Designing a hydroponic system that accommodates the needs of companion plants involves more than just throwing seeds into pods and filling up a water tank. It requires thoughtful consideration of each plant's growth habit and space requirements. Vertical towers or stacked trays are fantastic for small-footprint gardens and ideal for growing vining plants like peas or cucumbers alongside shorter, bushier plants like herbs. This not only maximizes the use of space but also ensures that each plant receives adequate light and air circulation, which are crucial for preventing disease and promoting vigorous growth.

Incorporating drip or nutrient film techniques (NFT) can also enhance your hydroponic companion planting system by delivering water and nutrients directly to each plant's roots. This precision feeding allows plants to absorb nutrients more efficiently, leading to faster growth and higher yields. However, it's essential to regularly check and maintain these systems to prevent clogs or leaks that could disrupt the flow of nutrients and water, potentially stressing your plants.

Pest and disease management in hydroponic systems requires vigilance and proactive strategies. Because these systems often involve a high density of plants and a moist environment, they can be particularly susceptible to outbreaks. Implementing integrated pest management (IPM) strategies such as introducing beneficial insects, using physical barriers like insect screens, or applying organic pesticides can help manage pests without compromising the health of your plants or the integrity of your system. Regularly inspecting your plants for signs of stress or disease can help you catch potential issues early and address them before they become severe.

Understanding and implementing these strategies can create a thriving hydroponic garden that produces abundant, healthy plants and exemplifies companion planting principles. Whether you are a seasoned hydroponic gardener or just starting, these techniques offer an exciting way to explore the synergy between different plants and their environment, leading to a more sustainable and productive gardening experience.

5.6 Succession Planting and Crop Rotation Strategies

In the tapestry of a well-maintained garden, every thread plays its part, intertwining in ways that enhance beauty and function. Succession planting and crop rotation are such threads, weaving through your garden's yearly cycle to ensure continuous production and maintain the health of the soil and plants. Structuring your garden with these methods in mind allows for an ongoing harvest supporting the environment and your dinner table.

Planning for Succession Planting

Succession planting is the gardener's strategy for making the garden produce continuously through the growing season. It involves planning multiple plantings of a single crop at intervals so that each reaches harvest at different times. You might, for instance, plant a row of lettuce every two weeks rather than all at once, ensuring a steady supply rather than a single, overwhelming harvest. This method maximizes the use of garden space. It keeps your soil actively engaged, which is particularly beneficial in companion planting setups where different plants can fulfil roles at other times, such as nitrogen-fixing legumes and preparing the soil for more nutrient-hungry crops later in the season.

Consider your plants' maturity period and seasonal preferences to implement this effectively. Cool-weather crops like spinach can be planted in early spring and again in late summer for a fall harvest. Meanwhile, fast-growing crops like radishes are perfect for filling in gaps and keeping the soil covered, while slower-growing neighbours like carrots prepare for their turn. When planning your garden's layout, allocate spaces that can be easily re-sown or replanted through the season, and keep a nursery area where seedlings can be started, ready to fill any unexpected gaps in your garden beds.

Benefits of Crop Rotation

Rotating crops each season is a time-honoured tradition with proven benefits for the companion garden. This practice helps manage soil fertility and control pests and diseases. Different plants have varying nutrient needs and pest associations. By rotating them, you prevent any one area of your garden from becoming a breeding ground for pests and diseases specific to a crop. Moreover, crop rotation prevents soil depletion, as different crops use and replenish nutrients at different rates. For instance, following a nitrogen-hungry crop like corn with a nitrogen-fixing crop like beans helps restore balance to the soil, making the need for chemical fertilizers redundant.

This rotation keeps the soil healthy and enhances your garden's biodiversity, making it more resilient to adverse conditions and improving overall plant health. The diversity discourages pests and diseases and can attract beneficial insects and birds, adding another layer of natural pest control.

Implementing Crop Rotation

Integrating crop rotation into a companion planting strategy does require a bit of planning but can be highly rewarding. A simple way to start is by categorizing plants into families and rotating them according to family. For example, avoid planting tomatoes in the same bed or plot where peppers, potatoes, or eggplants were grown the previous year since they belong to the same family and are susceptible to many of the same diseases.

Plan your garden in segments or beds, rotating each segment annually in a cycle. A four-year rotation is common, splitting crops into groups such as leafy greens, fruits (like tomatoes and peppers), roots, and legumes. Each group moves to a new segment each year, following a sequence that considers the specific needs and benefits of the crops involved; for instance, after legumes, which enrich the soil with nitrogen, plant leafy greens, which appreciate the extra nutrients, followed by fruiting plants, and then root crops, which can do well even as the soil nutrient levels start to decline.

Record-Keeping

Maintaining detailed records is crucial to succession planting and crop rotation success. You are keeping a garden journal or digital records where you note what was planted, where, when, and how it performed can provide invaluable insights over the years. Record specific varieties, planting and harvest dates, yield, and any issues with pests or diseases. This information will help you plan future gardens more effectively, allowing you to replicate successes and learn from failures.

These records become a personalized guide to your garden's rhythms and needs, helping you to fine-tune your planting schedule and crop rotation plans for optimal health and productivity. They can also be a delightful way to reflect on your garden's growth and change over the years, providing a practical and sentimental snapshot of your gardening journey.

In weaving the practices of succession planting and crop rotation into the fabric of your garden, you create a dynamic system that sustains and rejuvenates itself. By embracing these strategies, you ensure that your garden is a source of continual bounty and a resilient and self-sustaining ecosystem. As this chapter concludes, remember that each season brings new opportunities to refine these techniques, making each year in your garden more productive and enjoyable than the last.

As we turn our gardening pages from the structured strategies of planting and rotation, the next chapter will explore the art of blending traditional knowledge with modern techniques, continuing to enrich our understanding and mastery of the gardening craft.

SIX

Tackling Common Gardening Challenges

Every gardener faces their share of challenges, but think of them as opportunities to grow—not just your plants, but your skills and knowledge as a green thumb. In this chapter, we will quite literally explore the shady aspects of gardening. If you've ever struggled with dark corners of your garden where the sun seems to play hide and seek, you're not alone. Shade in the garden is often seen as a limitation, but it can be transformed into an asset with the right approach. Let's dive into the world of shade-loving plants and learn how to harmonize light and shadow to create a thriving garden sanctuary.

6.1 Dealing with Shade: Companion Plants That Thrive Together

Shade-Loving Companions

Shade in the garden does not spell the end of your planting ambitions. Many plants not only tolerate shade but thrive in it. Hostas, ferns, and astilbes are just a few plants that can flourish in lower light conditions. These plants can be wonderful companions in shaded areas, supporting each other in several ways. For instance, ferns can provide a humid microclimate that benefits astilbes, adding rich texture and colour to the understory of your garden. Another excellent pairing is between bleeding hearts and Solomon's seal. The arching stems of Solomon's seal contrast beautifully with the heart-shaped flowers of the bleeding hearts, creating a visually appealing composition that keeps weeds at bay under the canopy of taller trees or shrubs.

Maximizing Light

While embracing shade-loving plants is vital, maximizing whatever light is available is crucial. Strategic plant placement can make a significant difference. Consider the pattern of light and shadow throughout the day and season, and place taller plants in areas where they won't cast a shadow on shorter, light-sensitive species. Utilizing reflective surfaces such as white walls or placing garden mirrors can also help bounce light back into darker corners of the garden. This trick brightens the space and can make small shaded areas appear larger and more inviting.

Moisture Management

Managing moisture correctly in shaded areas is vital to avoiding common problems such as mould or rot. Shade often keeps the soil moist for longer, which can be beneficial but risky. To strike the right balance, incorporate organic mulch around your plants. Mulch helps retain moisture during dry spells and prevents oversaturation when it rains by absorbing excess water and releasing it slowly into the soil. This method is particularly effective in shaded gardens where evaporation is slower. Also, choose mulches like cedar bark, which is less likely to harbour mould or pests. Proper watering techniques also play a crucial role; water your shade garden in the morning to ensure the topsoil has enough time to dry out during the day, reducing the risk of fungal diseases.

Integrating Shade into Design

Integrate them into your design rather than fighting against shaded areas in your garden. Use these cooler, darker spaces to contrast brighter, sunlit areas. This can be done by using shade to highlight the colours and textures of plants that may look washed out in strong sunlight. For example, hostas' lush, deep greens can provide a stunning backdrop to the vibrant colours of sun-loving flowers planted at the edge of a shade border. Consider the aesthetic of pathways and seating areas in your garden design. A shaded nook with a bench surrounded by shade-loving perennials and ferns can become a tranquil retreat from the summer sun's heat, offering a peaceful spot to relax and enjoy the quieter side of nature.

By understanding the unique conditions that shaded areas present and choosing the right plants and strategies, you can transform these spaces into beautiful, productive parts of your garden. Embrace the shade as an opportunity to explore a different palette of plants and garden designs, enhancing the diversity and appeal of your outdoor sanctuary.

6.2 Soil Health: Companion Plants for Soil Rejuvenation

When you think about a garden, it's not just what you see above ground that matters. Beneath the surface, the soil is alive and bustling with activity, and it's the absolute powerhouse behind your garden's success. Healthy soil leads to healthy plants, and companion planting can significantly boost the vitality of your garden's foundation. Let's explore some incredible plants that do more than beautify—they rejuvenate and enrich the soil, making your garden a robust ecosystem.

Soil-Building Companions

Certain plants are not just good neighbours above the ground; they are also fantastic partners for improving soil health. Legumes, such as beans and peas, are well known for their ability to fix nitrogen in the soil, which is crucial for plant growth. You create a symbiotic relationship that feeds both plants by partnering these with nitrogen-loving plants like corn or spinach. Another great example is the dynamic duo of marigolds and tomatoes. Marigolds exude substances from their roots that can deter nematodes and other pests harmful to tomatoes. Beyond pest control, these substances also contribute to a healthier soil structure. Adding plants like comfrey, which has deep roots that mine the subsoil for nutrients, can bring up potassium, phosphorus, and calcium, making these nutrients available in the topsoil where shallower-rooted plants can benefit from them.

Cover Crops

Integrating cover crops into your garden is like giving your soil a spa treatment. Plants such as clover, vetch, and rye protect the soil from erosion and improve its structure and fertility. These plants can be sown during off-season times.

When the soil might otherwise be left bare, they protect against erosion and help maintain soil moisture levels. When tilled back into the soil at the end of their season, they provide organic matter and nutrients, significantly enhancing soil fertility. This process, often called "green manuring," can drastically reduce the need for chemical fertilizers, promoting a more organic gardening approach. For a companion planting twist, intersperse cover crops like clover around pathways or between rows of vegetables. They'll keep the weeds down and, at the same time, fix nitrogen in the soil, which will eventually benefit neighbouring plants.

Bioremediation Plants

As gardening enthusiasts and environmentalists, you have the power to rehabilitate contaminated soil using the remarkable ability of some plants, a process known as bioremediation. Sunflowers, for instance, can absorb toxins and heavy metals from the soil, making them excellent partners in gardens that might be rehabilitated or established on reclaimed sites. Planting these alongside other crops can gradually improve the health of the soil, making it viable for more sensitive plants in future growing seasons. Mustard plants are another great choice for their detoxifying effects, especially in beds previously treated with chemical pesticides or herbicides. These plants can be used as part of a rotational gardening strategy, cleansing the soil before planting more delicate vegetables and herbs.

Compost and Mulch

Discussion of soil health would only be complete with touching on the benefits of compost and mulch. Compost, rich in organic matter and beneficial microbes, is like gold for your garden. It adds essential nutrients to the soil and improves its structure, making it easier for roots to grow. Apply compost to your garden beds at the beginning and end of each growing season to keep the soil fertile and healthy. Mulching, meanwhile, is equally beneficial. Organic mulches such as straw or leaves help retain soil moisture, suppress weeds, and, over time, break down into compost, adding further to the soil's nutrient richness. For a companion planting strategy, consider using a living mulch—low-growing plants like thyme or creeping Charlie can cover bare soil between taller plants, reducing moisture loss and adding beauty while gradually improving the soil as they decompose.

Embracing these soil-enhancing strategies and plants ensures your garden remains a vibrant, productive space. Healthy soil leads to healthy plants, which leads to a bountiful harvest, so nurturing the ground beneath your feet is one of the most beneficial activities you can engage in as a gardener. Whether you're sowing cover crops, planting bioremediation, or enriching the earth with compost and mulch, each step towards improving soil health is a step towards a more flourishing garden.

6.3 Managing Overcrowding in Compact Spaces

When working with a limited garden area, the challenge isn't just growing your plants but growing them so they can all thrive without stepping on each other's roots. Managing space effectively in a compact garden requires a strategic approach, starting with selecting appropriate plants. Opt for varieties known for compact growth or those easily trained to use vertical space. For example, climbing peas and beans utilize vertical space beautifully, and when planted alongside shorter crops like spinach or radish, they effectively maximize ground and air space. Similarly, choosing dwarf varieties of typically larger plants, such as mini cabbages or patio tomatoes, can also help you make the most of your limited area without leading to a cramped environment.

Pruning and thinning are not just techniques; you are responsible as a gardener to prevent overcrowding, especially in small garden spaces where every inch counts. Regular pruning helps control plant size and encourages healthier, more productive growth. For instance, tomato plants can be pruned to maintain a manageable size while ensuring they still produce a plentiful harvest. Thinning, on the other hand, involves removing some plants to reduce density, which improves air circulation and reduces the risk of diseases. It's particularly important for root vegetables like carrots and beets, which need space to expand underground. By thinning out some seedlings early in the season, you allow the remaining plants enough room to develop fully.

The spatial arrangement of plants plays a crucial role in managing a compact garden. Employing square-foot gardening techniques, where the garden space is divided into small square sections, each dedicated to a different plant, can optimize your use of space and help manage plant growth effectively. This method not only makes it easier to plan and organize the garden but also simplifies maintenance tasks like weeding and harvesting. Companion planting can be effectively integrated into this system by pairing plants with beneficial relationships, such as tomatoes planted next to basil, which helps to repel pests naturally while enhancing the flavour of the tomatoes.

Container and raised bed gardening are excellent solutions for managing space in compact areas. Containers are incredibly versatile and can be moved to make the best use of available sunlight. This is particularly useful in small spaces with varying light conditions throughout the day and season. Raised beds, meanwhile, provide a defined growing area that can help manage soil quality and prevent the spread of weeds and pests from surrounding areas. Both methods allow for better control over the growing environment and can be tailored to the plant's needs. For instance, deeper containers can accommodate root vegetables, while shallow trays might be perfect for herbs and leafy greens.

By carefully selecting the right plants, employing pruning and thinning techniques, arranging your space strategically, and utilizing containers and raised beds, you can effectively manage and even prevent overcrowding in your compact garden. These strategies help maximize your growing space and ensure that each plant has enough room to thrive, leading to a healthier, more bountiful garden.

6.4 Companion Planting to Attract Beneficial Insects

Imagine your garden not just as a collection of plants but as a vibrant community of beneficial insects, each playing a crucial role in maintaining a healthy ecosystem. These tiny allies, nature's pest control agents, pollinators, and soil enhancers, are there because you chose the right plants. You can invite these beneficial insects into your garden, creating a dynamic environment where natural balances maintain plant health and productivity. In this section, we'll delve into attracting beneficial bugs with companion planting, creating inviting habitats, balancing their populations, and observing their interactions to manage your garden ecosystem effectively.

Beneficial Insect Attractors

By attracting beneficial insects to your garden, you add beauty and diversity and implement a natural pest control system. Certain plants, with their specific colours, shapes, or nectars, act as magnets for these insects. Flowers such as yarrow, sweet alyssum, and cosmos are fantastic for attracting a wide range of beneficial insects, including ladybugs, lacewings, and hoverflies. These insects feed on common pests such as aphids and caterpillars, naturally reducing your need for chemical interventions. Herbs also play a significant role in attracting beneficial bugs; for example, dill and fennel are particularly good at attracting wasps that parasitize pest caterpillars, and their umbrella-shaped flowers are perfect for tiny beneficial insects that sip nectar or pollen. By planting a mix of these, you create a buffet for beneficial insects, which not only helps in pest control but also aids in pollinating your garden crops.

Creating Habitats for Beneficial Insects

Creating a habitat for beneficial insects is not just a hobby; it's a significant contribution to environmental conservation. It's about understanding and meeting the insects' lifecycle needs from larvae to adults. Many beneficial insects, such as ladybugs and lacewings, lay their eggs in sheltered spaces where their larvae can safely grow and access food. You can facilitate this by leaving some areas of your garden a little wilder, with layers of leaves or loosely stacked branches to provide hiding spots. Additionally, consider incorporating perennial plants with hollow stems, such as raspberries or elderberries, which can offer overwintering habitats for adult insects. Considering the full lifecycle of these beneficial creatures, you provide a year-round home, ensuring they are present in your garden across different seasons to perform their essential roles.

Balancing Insect Populations

While beneficial insects are key allies in the garden, their populations need to be balanced to prevent them from becoming pests themselves. This balance can be achieved by diversifying the plant species in your garden, which helps ensure that no single insect population can dominate. Planting various flowering plants is crucial as it ensures a steady supply of nectar throughout the growing season, keeping beneficial insect populations stable and active. Introducing plants that attract predatory insects can also help keep herbivore populations in check. For instance, planting marigolds to attract hoverflies can help control aphid outbreaks. Regular monitoring and being responsive to changes in insect activity can help you maintain this balance, making slight adjustments to plantings or habitats as needed.

Observation and Management

Observation is your best tool in managing the garden's ecosystem. Spend time observing the interactions between different insects and plants in your garden. Notice which plants attract specific insects and whether these insects contribute to reducing pest populations or aiding in pollination. This hands-on knowledge can help you make informed decisions about which plants to add or remove, optimizing the ecological balance in your garden. Keep a garden journal to record your observations, including details of insect sightings, plant health, and the effectiveness of different plant combinations. This record-keeping will be invaluable, helping you refine your strategies and develop a deeper understanding of your garden's intricate web of life.

By embracing these practices, you turn your garden into a thriving habitat for beneficial insects, enhancing your space's health and beauty. Remember, each insect that visits your garden plays a part in its ecological story, contributing to a complex and vibrant tapestry of life that supports your gardening goals.

6.5 Drought-Tolerant Companion Planting

Cultivating a lush garden can seem like a mirage in regions where the rain is as scarce as a cloudless desert sky. However, you can create an oasis that thrives in dry conditions with the right approach. Drought-tolerant companion planting is not just about surviving the dry spells; it's about creating a symbiotic garden environment where plants support each other in conserving moisture and maximizing resilience. Let's delve into the world of drought-resistant companions and uncover how they can help each other and your garden prosper even when water is limited.

Choosing species that naturally require less water is crucial when selecting plants that can withstand arid conditions. For instance, succulents like sedums and sempervivums store moisture in their leaves and thrive in dry soil. These can be paired with deep-rooted plants such as lavender and rosemary, which can access water from deeper soil layers. This combination allows you to cover different soil depths for moisture, ensuring that your garden utilizes water efficiently without one plant robbing another of this precious resource. Another excellent pairing involves using native plants naturally adapted to your local climate's dry conditions. For example, pairing prairie coneflower with native grasses can create a resilient mini-ecosystem that supports local wildlife while requiring minimal additional watering.

Advanced water conservation techniques are vital in managing a drought-tolerant garden. One effective method is drip irrigation systems, which deliver water directly to the base of the plants. This technique minimizes evaporation and runoff, ensuring that every drop of water is used effectively. Drip irrigation can be automated with timers, making water management efficient and convenient, especially in regions with strict water use regulations. Additionally, grouping plants with similar water needs together ensures that each section of your garden receives just the right amount of irrigation without overwatering some plants while underwatering others.

Mulching plays a pivotal role in conserving moisture. Using organic mulches such as straw, bark, or shredded leaves helps retain soil moisture and adds nutrients as they decompose. For a drought-tolerant garden, consider using heavier mulches like gravel or rocks, which do an excellent job of retaining moisture without absorbing it. These materials also reflect heat away from the soil, reducing moisture evaporation. When applying mulch, ensure it's spread evenly around plants without touching the stems to prevent rotting and to allow slow percolation of water into the soil whenever watering does occur.

Designing a garden that maximizes water efficiency involves more than just plant selection and mulching; it requires a strategic layout that considers the flow and conservation of water. Creating a garden with slight slopes can help manage water runoff, directing it towards plants that need it most. Incorporating swales or shallow ditches lined with drought-resistant plants can capture runoff and use it efficiently. Additionally, placing thirstier plants in areas where water naturally accumulates, such as near downspouts or in lower parts of your garden, can use available water without additional resources. In this way, every part of your garden contributes to a holistic system where water is utilized to its fullest potential, no matter how scarce.

By adopting these strategies and embracing the natural resilience of drought-tolerant plants, your garden can become a testament to nature's beauty and endurance. It's about creating a landscape that survives and thrives under challenging conditions, proving that even in dry climates, your gardening aspirations need not dry up.

6.6 Cold-Climate Companion Planting Strategies

Navigating the chilly challenges of a cold-climate garden might seem daunting, but with suitable companions, your garden can survive and thrive through frosty temperatures. The benefits of these strategies are immense, as plants like kale, Brussels sprouts, and parsnips are not merely survivors of the cold; they become sweeter after a frost. Pairing these with mulch-producing plants like oats or barley can protect the soil from freezing too quickly while providing a natural blanket that keeps these cold-hardy companions cosy. Garlic is another robust choice. When planted near roses, it can help deter pests while withstanding the cold, thanks to its hardy nature.

Creating and utilizing microclimates within your garden is like crafting little pockets of ideal growing conditions that can significantly extend the viability of your plantings. One effective way to manipulate microclimates is by using the thermal mass of stone walls or patio floors, which absorb heat during the day and radiate it back during the cooler nights, providing a warmer micro-environment. This can be a perfect spot for a cold-sensitive plant surrounded by hardier plants that don't need the extra warmth but can benefit from the sheltered position. Strategic placement of windbreaks made from shrubs or tall plants can also shield more delicate companions from cold winds, reducing wind chill and the risk of frost damage.

As the growing season in cold climates can be frustratingly short, implementing season extension techniques can offer a lifeline. Cold frames, which are essentially miniature greenhouses, can be a game-changer. By constructing a simple framework around your plants and covering it with a clear lid, you can keep many plants growing well into the colder months. Mulching with straw or leaves can also help insulate the soil, keeping the ground warmer and extending root growth times before the deep freeze sets in. These techniques not only prolong your gardening season but also increase the yield and health of your plants, giving them a robust start in the spring or a prolonged life in the fall.

Winter planning is crucial in cold climates for protecting your plants and setting the stage for the next growing season. When selecting plants, look for varieties known for their ability to withstand freezing temperatures. Plants like winter rye or wheat can be sown in late fall; they not only survive the winter but also rejuvenate the soil as they decompose in the spring, providing a nutrient-rich environment for new plantings. Additionally, consider the architecture of your garden—raised beds can be particularly effective in cold climates as they drain better and warm up faster in the spring, which can be a boon for early sowing.

By integrating these cold-climate strategies into your garden planning, you're preparing to survive the winter and actively creating a garden that utilizes every possible advantage to extend its productive months. This proactive approach ensures that your garden remains a vibrant, thriving entity year-round despite the challenges posed by a colder climate.

As we wrap up this chapter, remember that each cold-climate garden is a unique ecosystem. Your success lies in selecting the proper plant companions, creating protective microclimates, extending your growing season, and meticulously planning for winter. These strategies are about enduring the cold months and embracing and utilizing them to enhance your garden's growth cycle and productivity.

The next chapter will explore combining traditional wisdom and modern techniques to enhance gardening success. This blend of old and new perspectives will enrich your understanding and expand your toolkit as a gardener, ensuring that your garden grows in beauty and bounty through every season.

SEVEN

Companion Planting for Specific Goals

I magine walking through your garden, watching your plants flourish together, creating a lush tapestry of greenery that's not just beautiful but incredibly productive. This isn't just a daydream; it's entirely achievable with the strategic use of companion planting tailored to maximize your garden's yield. In this chapter, we're diving deep into how you can enhance your garden's productivity by carefully selecting plant partners that work together to boost each other's growth and output. Whether you're a seasoned gardener or just starting out, these insights will help you transform your green space into a productivity powerhouse.

7.1 Companion Planting for Maximum Yield

Intensive Planting Strategies

Maximizing garden productivity often starts with making the most of the space available. Intensive planting strategies, a cornerstone of effective companion planting, allow you to grow more in less space while ensuring each plant supports its neighbours' growth. One popular method is the square foot gardening technique, where the garden is divided into small square segments, each meticulously planned to host different plants based on their size and needs. This method reduces wasted space and can significantly increase yield per square foot.

Another strategy is intercropping, where you plant quick-growing crops alongside slower-growing ones. For example, radishes and carrots are great companions—they grow quickly, breaking the soil and making it easier for the slower-growing carrots to expand. When the carrots need more room, the radishes are harvested, leaving just the right amount of space for the carrots to flourish. This method optimises space and ensures a continuous harvest of different crops from the same bed, making your garden a constant source of fresh produce.

Vertical gardening is another excellent way to enhance yield, especially if you're short on space. Utilizing vertical space with trellises, poles, or climbing frames allows you to grow vining crops like peas, beans, and cucumbers upwards, freeing up precious ground space for other plants. This increases your garden's yield and promotes better air circulation and sunlight exposure, leading to healthier plants and bigger harvests.

Nutrient Sharing Combinations

The magic of companion planting also lies in its ability to pair plants to share or complement each other's nutrient needs. A classic example is the time-honoured combination of corn, beans, and squash, often called the "Three Sisters." In this trio, the beans fix nitrogen in the soil, which is beneficial for the nitrogen-loving corn, while the squash spreads along the ground, shading the soil, conserving moisture, and suppressing weeds. This reduces the need for fertilizers and watering and naturally enhances the growth and yield of all three crops, making the "Three Sisters" a cornerstone of sustainable gardening practices.

Another effective pairing is tomatoes and basil. Besides the well-known flavour benefits basil brings to tomatoes, basil helps improve the overall health of the tomatoes. It can enhance the taste and yield of tomatoes by repelling harmful pests and attracting beneficial insects. Plus, planting basil between tomato plants can help maximize space and increase the overall productivity of your garden.

Success Stories

Real-world examples can provide powerful inspiration and practical insights into the effectiveness of these strategies. Consider the story of a community garden that implemented companion planting across its entire plot. Intensive planting techniques and nutrient-sharing combinations could double their vegetable output in a single season. Tomatoes planted alongside basil and marigolds yielded healthier fruit and had fewer pest infestations compared to previous seasons when they were grown alone.

Another success story comes from a small urban garden that used vertical planting to maximize its limited space. Growing beans and cucumbers on trellises above their salad greens, which thrive in partial shade, the gardeners could harvest fresh salads throughout the summer without the greens bolting from too much sun. This clever use of space and understanding of plant needs led to an abundant harvest from a small footprint, inspiring neighbours to adopt similar strategies.

Continuous Harvest Tips

Timing and succession planting are crucial to ensuring a continuous harvest. Plan your garden so that as one crop is harvested, another is ready to take its place. For instance, once early-season radishes are harvested, plant a batch of beans in the same space, which will benefit from the loosened soil. Keep a garden calendar to track planting and harvesting times, and feel free to adjust based on what you learn each season.

Additionally, transplants should be considered instead of seeds for some crops to shorten the harvest time. This can be particularly useful for slower-growing vegetables like tomatoes or peppers, ensuring a continuous output of produce throughout the growing season. By planning carefully and adjusting as you learn, you can create a garden that looks great and provides a steady supply of fresh produce from spring to fall.

By implementing these strategies, you can transform your garden into a productive oasis that yields an impressive harvest and brings joy and satisfaction. Whether filling your kitchen with fresh herbs and vegetables or sharing your bounty with neighbours, these companion planting techniques offer a practical and rewarding way to enhance your gardening success.

7.2 Building a Pollinator-Friendly Garden

Creating a garden that buzzes with life, where bees, butterflies, and other beneficial insects flit from flower to flower, is not just about beauty—it's about sustaining a thriving ecosystem in your backyard. Pollinators play a crucial role in the health of our planet, aiding in the production of fruits, vegetables, and seeds. By selecting the right plants and designing your garden with these tiny visitors in mind, you can create a sanctuary that supports their health and ensures their presence year-round.

Selecting Pollinator-Attractive Plants

Begin with choosing plants known to attract a broad spectrum of pollinators. Flowers like lavender, cosmos, and zinnias are excellent at drawing bees due to their colourful and nectar-rich blossoms. For butterflies, plants such as milkweed, butterfly bush, and goldenrod provide both nectar for adults and habitat for larvae. Remember about herbs; many flowering herbs like thyme, sage, and oregano are also fantastic for attracting bees while adding versatility to your garden. Planting a variety of these, with staggered blooming times, ensures that pollinators can access nectar from early spring through late fall. Additionally, incorporating native plants is particularly effective as these species have evolved alongside local pollinators and are often well-suited to meeting their needs.

Designing for Pollinators

When planning your garden layout, consider making the space inviting and accessible to pollinators. Grouping plants in clusters can create a "target" for pollinators, making it easier for them to find the flowers. Additionally, various plant heights and types add visual interest and cater to pollinator species. For instance, some bees prefer to forage near the ground, while others may be more attracted to taller blooms. Incorporating elements such as shallow water basins or a pile of small stones can provide essential drinking spots for bees and butterflies, ensuring they spend more time in your garden. Paths lined with low-growing lavender or thyme can also encourage pollinators to linger and explore further, enhancing the overall health of your garden by ensuring thorough pollination.

Supporting Pollinator Health

The health of pollinators is paramount, and companion planting offers a natural way to support their well-being. Avoiding the use of pesticides is a critical first step, as these chemicals can be harmful or even lethal to many pollinators. Instead, foster a balanced ecosystem where plants naturally repel pests and attract beneficial insects. For example, marigolds emit a scent that can deter harmful insects while attracting pollinators with their bright flowers. Additionally, practising crop rotation and planting a diverse array of plants can help prevent disease and pest outbreaks that might otherwise affect pollinator populations. Providing nesting sites, such as bee hotels for solitary bees, or maintaining areas with dead wood and leaf litter for beetles and butterflies, can also enhance pollinator health by offering safe places for breeding and overwintering.

Year-Round Pollinator Support

Planning for continuous bloom ensures your garden supports pollinators throughout the year. Early spring flowers like crocuses and snowdrops provide critical nectar sources when food is scarce. Transitioning into summer, plants such as echinacea and bee balm keep the garden vibrant and active. As autumn approaches, late bloomers like asters and sedums offer sustenance well into the cooler months. Additionally, consider planting evergreen shrubs or trees to provide shelter during harsh weather. By thoughtfully selecting plants that offer overlapping bloom periods, you ensure that your garden remains a haven for pollinators no matter the season, supporting their lifecycle and contributing to the health of your local ecosystem year-round.

Through these strategies, your garden can become a vital pollinator refuge, enriching the local biodiversity and bringing your outdoor space to life with the sights and sounds of nature's best pollinators. This enhances the beauty and productivity of your garden and contributes to the more significant effort to support and sustain pollinator populations essential to our global ecology.

7.3 Companion Plants for Natural Pest Control

Imagine strolling through your garden, admiring the blooms but also noticing fewer pests than ever before. This isn't due to heavy pesticide use but rather the strategic choice of companion plants that naturally keep your garden healthier and more resilient. In organic gardening, harnessing the power of certain plants to deter pests or attract beneficial predators is a game-changer. Let's explore how integrating biological pest control plants into your garden layout can create a self-regulating ecosystem that naturally manages pests.

Plants like chives emit a subtle but potent odour and can be excellent companions for roses, deterring aphids that otherwise feast on rose bushes. Similarly, with their vibrant blooms, nasturtiums add a splash of colour and serve as trap crops for aphids, drawing them away from more vulnerable plants. Garlic is more than just a kitchen staple; when planted near fruit trees, its strong scent masks the trees from pests like borers and can reduce fungal infections. These biological pest control plants work by repelling harmful pests with their strong scents or attracting them away from main crops, acting as sacrificial plants.

Creating a balanced garden ecosystem goes beyond just planting a few pest-repellent plants. It involves understanding the relationships between different plant species and how they interact with each other and the environment. For instance, planting a mix of flowering plants among your vegetables can attract a host of beneficial insects that pollinate the plants and prey on pests. Ladybugs, lacewings, and parasitic wasps are all attracted to sweet alyssum, cosmos, and marigolds. These beneficial insects help keep pest populations under control, reducing the need for chemical interventions.

One inspiring case study involves a community garden that faced a severe aphid infestation. The gardeners introduced several rows of marigolds and nasturtiums alongside their vegetable plots. Within weeks, they noticed a significant reduction in aphids, attributed to the marigolds attracting ladybugs, natural predators of aphids, and the nasturtiums acting as a trap crop. This natural intervention controlled the aphid problem and increased the overall yield and health of the vegetable crops.

Moreover, companion planting fits seamlessly into an Integrated Pest Management (IPM) strategy, which advocates for a holistic approach to pest control. IPM emphasizes the importance of maintaining ecological balance and using pest control methods that are least disruptive to garden ecosystems. Companion planting contributes to IPM by reducing the reliance on chemical pesticides, fostering biodiversity, and enhancing the natural resilience of the garden. By observing and intervening only when necessary and choosing plant combinations that support natural pest management, gardeners can maintain a healthy garden ecosystem with minimal impact on the surrounding environment.

By embracing these strategies, you are not just preventing pests; you are cultivating a garden that is a dynamic, interconnected ecosystem. This approach promotes a healthier garden and aligns with sustainable gardening practices that benefit the wider environment. As you plan your garden, consider these companion plants and strategies as essential tools in your gardening toolkit, helping you grow beautiful but also resilient and productive plants.

7.4 Companion Planting for Herbal Gardens

Creating a herbal garden that's both bountiful and beautiful is about more than just planting your favourite herbs. It's about understanding how different herbs can benefit each other, enhancing growth, flavour, and medicinal qualities. This nurturing approach leads to healthier plants and ensures a richer harvest of aromatic leaves for your kitchen and apothecary. Let's explore how to pair herbs for enhanced growth, boost their essential oil content, integrate them with vegetables for mutual benefits, and design an herb garden that becomes a hub of productivity and vitality.

Herb Pairings for Enhanced Growth

Choosing the right herb combinations can make all the difference in companion planting in an herbal garden. For instance, basil and parsley can be planted together because they share similar light and water requirements and can help each other flourish. Basil is known to improve the flavour and growth of parsley, while parsley, in turn, provides ground cover to help maintain soil moisture that benefits basil. Another excellent pairing is chives and rosemary. Chives can deter pests that typically affect rosemary, while the strong scent of rosemary can enhance the aromatic oils in chives, making them more potent. Additionally, planting cilantro and dill together can be beneficial as both herbs attract beneficial insects that help control pests that could affect their growth. Understanding and implementing these herb pairings allows you to create a symbiotic environment where your herbs survive and thrive.

Maximizing Essential Oil Production

The quality of a herb is often measured by the potency of its essential oils, which are responsible for its flavour and therapeutic properties. To maximize these qualities, consider the soil and companions of your herbs. For instance, lavender planted near oregano can benefit from the oregano's natural ability to repel common pests, resulting in healthier lavender plants with more concentrated essential oils. Similarly, mint can produce exceptionally aromatic leaves when grown in partial shade and paired with companion plants like chamomile, which enhances its growth and oil content. It's also beneficial to occasionally trim these herbs, as pruning encourages the plants to produce more oils to protect new growth, leading to a more potent harvest.

Another tip is to consider the timing of your harvest. Herbs should generally be picked right before flowering when their oil concentrations peak. This practice ensures you're using the leaves at their most flavorful and medicinally effective. Combining these harvesting techniques with strategic companion planting can significantly boost your herbs' essential oil production, enhancing their culinary and medicinal value.

Herbal Companion Plants for Vegetables

Herbs can be more than just seasonings; they can also play an integral role in the health and productivity of your vegetable garden. For example, planting basil among your tomatoes can help to repel harmful insects like thrips and flies, while the strong scent of garlic can deter pests from nibbling on lettuce and other leafy greens. Additionally, herbs like dill and fennel attract beneficial insects that prey on common vegetable pests, providing a natural form of pest control that can keep your vegetable garden thriving.

Moreover, certain herbs can improve the flavour of vegetables when planted nearby. This phenomenon, known as allelopathy, involves certain compounds that herbs release into the soil, which can subtly affect the flavour profile of neighbouring vegetables. For instance, planting chervil near radishes can make the radishes crisper and spicier, while sage can enhance the sweetness of carrots. By thoughtfully integrating herbs into your vegetable garden, you can bolster your garden's health and yield and enrich the flavours of your harvest, making every meal a gourmet experience.

Designing a Companion Herb Garden

Designing a herb garden that effectively utilizes companion planting requires a thoughtful approach. Consider your chosen herbs' light, water, and soil preferences. Group herbs with similar needs together to simplify care and ensure each plant gets the right resources. For example, Mediterranean herbs such as thyme, rosemary, and oregano thrive in full sun and well-drained soil and can be planted together in a sunny part of the garden.

Incorporate different heights and growth habits to use space and create visual interest fully. Taller herbs like fennel can be a backdrop for lower-growing, spreading herbs like thyme. Consider also using borders or pathways lined with low-growing herbs such as creeping thyme or chamomile, which can withstand light foot traffic and release a delightful fragrance when brushed against.

Lastly, rotate your herbs annually, especially if you're planting annuals like basil or cilantro. This practice prevents soil depletion and reduces the buildup of pests and diseases that can accumulate when the same plants are grown in the same spots year after year. With careful planning and a bit of creativity, your herb garden can become a testament to the principles of companion planting, showcasing not only the beauty of these versatile plants but also their ability to support each other for a bountiful, aromatic harvest.

7.5 Edible Flowers and Companion Planting

Edible flowers bring a splash of colour and a burst of flavour to any garden, but their benefits extend far beyond their visual appeal and taste. When selecting edible flowers to incorporate into your garden, consider varieties that offer culinary versatility and companion benefits. Nasturtiums, for instance, are vibrant and peppery and excel at attracting pollinators and deterring pests like aphids and cucumber beetles. With its sunny blooms, Calendula is another excellent choice; it's known for its healing properties and can help enhance soil health by attracting beneficial insects. With its striking blue flowers, Borage attracts bees and can improve the growth and flavour of strawberries and tomatoes when planted nearby.

The culinary uses of edible flowers are vast and exciting. With their bright petals and spicy flavour, nasturtiums make a stunning addition to salads and can be a delightful pesto. Lavender, known for its soothing aroma, can be used to add a floral note to baked goods or steeped to create a calming tea. For their mild, grassy flavour, consider pansies, perfect for garnishing cocktails or decorating cakes. Incorporating these flowers into your cooking elevates the aesthetics of your dishes and infuses them with unique flavours that can't be replicated with other ingredients.

Edible flowers also offer dual benefits in the garden. Aesthetically, they add a layer of beauty that enhances the overall look of your garden, making it not just a place of cultivation but also a sanctuary of beauty. Functionally, many edible flowers play significant roles in the health of your garden. For example, stunning and edible sunflowers act as natural trellises for climbing plants such as beans and cucumbers, providing them with the support they need to thrive. Furthermore, the giant heads of sunflowers can attract birds, which help control insect populations by feeding on pests.

The role of edible flowers in attracting pollinators cannot be overstated. Flowers like marigolds and zinnias add beauty to your garden and serve as powerful magnets for bees, butterflies, and other pollinators. Their presence increases the biodiversity of your garden, which is crucial for maintaining ecological balance and ensuring that your fruits and vegetables are well-pollinated. This leads to better crop yields and more robust plant growth. Thoughtfully choosing and positioning edible flowers throughout your garden creates a vibrant ecosystem where plants and pollinators thrive, ensuring your garden is as healthy as beautiful.

You can enjoy their culinary benefits and functional advantages by integrating edible flowers into your garden through thoughtful selection and strategic placement. These blossoms bring life to your dishes and vitality to your garden, embodying what makes companion planting a genuinely holistic approach to gardening. Whether used for their beauty, taste, or companion benefits, edible flowers offer a unique opportunity to enhance your gardening experience's productivity and pleasure.

7.6 Companion Planting for Medicinal Plants

Growing medicinal plants isn't just about having ready access to natural remedies; it's also about understanding the relationships between these plants and their companions, which can significantly enhance their growth and medicinal qualities. For instance, consider the pairing of echinacea and yarrow. Echinacea is widely valued for its immune-boosting properties, while yarrow is known for its ability to heal wounds. When planted together, yarrow can help attract beneficial insects that protect echinacea from pests, thus enhancing its growth and potency. Additionally, yarrow's deep roots bring up subsoil nutrients, benefiting echinacea with shallower roots. This mutual support strengthens their medicinal properties and ensures a healthier garden.

Creating an environment where these plants can thrive is crucial when crafting a garden that focuses on medicinal plants. Start with the soil, the foundation of your garden's health. Medicinal plants such as lavender and chamomile thrive in well-drained soil, while others, like marshmallows, require more moisture-retentive conditions. Amending your soil with organic matter can improve its structure and nutrient content, supporting the diverse needs of your medicinal garden. Also, consider the pH requirements of each plant. For example, lavender prefers slightly alkaline soil, whereas blueberry plants, which have specific medicinal uses, thrive in acidic conditions. Testing your soil and adjusting its pH can significantly affect the effectiveness and yield of your medicinal plants.

The right amount of sunlight is another critical factor. Most medicinal herbs, such as basil and thyme, need full sun to develop their best flavours and medicinal compounds. However, some, like gotu kola and goldenseal, benefit from partial shade, especially in hotter climates. Design your garden so each plant receives the optimal light for specific needs. This might mean planting taller plants on the north side of your garden to provide the necessary shade for smaller, more delicate herbs. Observing how the sun moves across your space and adjusting your plant placements accordingly can significantly boost the medicinal qualities of your herbs.

Harvesting and Usage Tips

Harvesting your medicinal plants at the right time maximises their healing potential. Generally, the best time to harvest most herbs is before they flower, when their essential oils and medicinal compounds are most concentrated. Autumn is the best time for harvesting roots like dandelion and burdock, as the plants have had the whole season to gather nutrients. When harvesting leaves, do so in the morning after the dew has dried but before the sun is at its peak to ensure that the essential oils are still potent.

Once harvested, knowing how to dry and store your medicinal plants properly will ensure that they retain their therapeutic properties. Herbs can be air-dried in a dark, well-ventilated area or using a dehydrator at a low temperature. Store dried herbs in airtight containers away from light and heat, which can degrade their quality. When using these herbs, whether for teas, tinctures, or topical applications, always refer to guidelines on effective dosages and consult a healthcare provider, mainly if you use them for specific health issues.

Creating a healing garden with companion plants offers a beautiful, functional space that promotes health and well-being. By understanding and implementing the principles of companion planting, you're not just growing plants; you're cultivating a living pharmacy right in your backyard.

As this chapter on medicinal plants concludes, remember that the key to a successful medicinal garden lies in understanding the specific needs of each plant and how they interact with their neighbours. This knowledge not only enhances the health and yield of your garden but also ensures that you have access to potent, effective remedies. The principles covered here pave the way for more sustainable and self-sufficient living, connecting us deeply to the natural world and its healing properties.

Moving forward, the next chapter will explore the integration of technology in modern gardening, showing how traditional practices can merge with new innovations to create even more dynamic and productive gardens. This blend of old and new enriches our gardening practices, ensuring they remain relevant and effective in our changing world.

EIGHT

The Future of Companion Planting

As you've begun cultivating your companion-planted garden, you've tapped into an age-old practice that's as dynamic as sustainable. But what does the future hold for companion planting? With innovations in technology, ongoing global practices, and the challenges posed by environmental changes, the landscape of companion planting is ever-evolving. Let's explore these horizons together, discovering how modern advancements and global insights are shaping the future of gardening.

8.1 Innovations in Companion Planting

Technology and Companion Planting

In an era where technology touches almost every aspect of our lives, gardening is no exception. Recent advancements have brought us a variety of apps designed to simplify and enhance companion planting. Imagine an app that helps you track your garden plants' growth, health, and needs while suggesting optimal companion plants based on your specific garden conditions. These apps use data from your garden to provide tailored advice, making it easier to manage your space efficiently. They can alert you about the best times to plant, water, and harvest, taking much of the guesswork out of gardening. This integration of technology not only streamlines garden management but also makes companion planting more accessible, especially for beginners like you who might feel overwhelmed by the complexities of starting a new garden.

Research and Development

Behind the scenes, scientists and horticulturists continuously explore the interactions between different plant species. This ongoing research is uncovering new benefits of companion planting, such as enhanced resistance to pests and diseases, improved soil health, and even better flavour profiles of fruits and vegetables. For instance, recent studies have shown that certain plant combinations can significantly boost soil nutrients, increasing the nutritional value of the crops grown in that soil. These discoveries validate the benefits of companion planting and open up new possibilities for optimizing plant pairings to achieve specific goals, whether it's maximizing yield, conserving water, or enhancing the nutritional content of the plants.

Global Practices

As we look around the world, innovative companion planting practices are being implemented across different climates and cultures, offering a rich source of knowledge and inspiration. In tropical regions, farmers are using companion planting to effectively manage pest control without resorting to harmful pesticides. For example, in some parts of Africa, maize is planted alongside beans and squash—a method similar to the "Three Sisters" practised by Native Americans. This maximizes land use and improves soil fertility and crop productivity. Learning from such global practices broadens our understanding of companion planting and encourages adaptation and experimentation in our gardens.

Future Challenges

Looking ahead, companion planting faces challenges like climate change and biodiversity loss, which threaten the delicate balance of our ecosystems. As weather patterns become more unpredictable, choosing and managing plant pairings that can withstand extreme conditions will be crucial. Companion planting can play a vital role by enhancing plant resilience and creating more diverse, sustainable garden ecosystems that can better withstand such challenges. Moreover, as urbanization continues to reduce natural habitats, our gardens, especially those incorporating companion planting principles, will be vital sanctuaries for supporting biodiversity and providing refuge for various insects, birds, and wildlife.

In this ever-changing world, the principles of companion planting remain a beacon for sustainable gardening practices, guiding us toward a future where our gardens not only thrive but also contribute to the health of our planet. As you nurture your garden, consider these innovations and global insights as tools and inspiration to enhance your gardening journey, making every plant choice a step toward a more sustainable and resilient future.

8.2 Community and Social Aspects of Companion Planting

Community gardens embody more than just shared spaces for planting; they forge bonds among neighbours, creating networks of relationships and mutual assistance that extend far beyond the garden itself. Companion planting emerges as a horticultural method and a powerful metaphor for community life in these vibrant green spaces. When different plants thrive together, they create a more robust ecosystem, just as diverse groups of people can enrich a community. For example, in a community garden, tomatoes might be grown next to basil and marigolds, which help repel pests and enhance each other's growth. This cooperative relationship between plants can mirror and encourage collaborative relationships among gardeners, who share tips, tools, and the fruits of their labour.

The social cohesion fostered by community gardens can be particularly impactful in urban areas, where green spaces are scarce, and neighbours might otherwise have few opportunities to interact. These gardens become gathering places where people of all ages and backgrounds come together, united by a common interest in gardening. They discuss the growth of their plants, exchange gardening tips, and celebrate harvests together, strengthening community ties and fostering a sense of belonging and mutual responsibility. The collaborative nature of companion planting, requiring understanding and coordination between gardeners, reinforces these social bonds and teaches the values of cooperation and sustainability.

Sharing knowledge is another cornerstone of the companion planting community. Seasoned gardeners often take it upon themselves to guide beginners, imparting wisdom on everything from the best companion plants for local conditions to natural methods for pest control. This mentorship helps new gardeners succeed and perpetuates a cycle of learning and sharing that keeps the community vibrant. Workshops and informal garden chats can be instrumental in spreading this knowledge and helping everyone in the community improve their practices. Moreover, experienced gardeners might share seeds or cuttings of their favourite companion plants, which helps preserve plant varieties and gardening techniques that might otherwise be lost.

Educational opportunities abound in the realm of companion planting. Schools and community programs can integrate gardening into their curriculums to teach lessons in biology, ecology, responsibility, nutrition, and environmental stewardship. Students can see firsthand how plants like beans and corn support each other while learning about Native American agricultural practices and sustainable farming. Such programs provide practical gardening skills and help young people understand the importance of caring for the environment and how ecosystems function. The hands-on nature of gardening, combined with the strategic thinking involved in companion planting, makes it an excellent educational tool that engages students in a way that traditional classroom settings may not.

The rise of social media and gardening networks has also played a pivotal role in spreading companion planting innovations and stories. Platforms like Instagram and Pinterest are filled with vibrant photos and posts where gardeners worldwide share their successes and challenges with companion planting. These digital communities provide spaces where ideas can flourish and inspire others to try new planting combinations or solve gardening problems creatively. Blogs and gardening forums allow for more profound knowledge exchanges, from detailed plant care guides to discussions on the latest eco-friendly gardening trends. This global exchange of information enriches individual gardening practices and fosters a sense of international community among gardeners united by their shared commitment to nurturing the earth.

Participating in these vibrant community and social exchanges—whether in local gardens, classrooms, or online forums—makes you part of a more significant movement towards sustainable living and environmental awareness. With its deep roots in cooperation and mutual benefit, Companion planting offers a perfect metaphor for the interdependent relationships that make our communities thrive. As you tend to your garden, remember that each plant, like each person, brings something unique to the ecosystem, and it's by working together we create a healthier, more sustainable world.

8.3 Companion Planting as a Family Activity

Engaging children in gardening, primarily through companion planting, transforms your garden into a vibrant classroom where ecology, biology, and teamwork lessons naturally sprout from the soil. To make this a delightful experience for the little ones:

1. Start with tasks that feel more like play than work.
2. Let them handle seeds, perhaps the large, easy-to-grasp ones like beans and pumpkins.
3. Show them how to nestle these seeds into the soil, explaining how each seed will wake up and grow into a plant with the right mix of soil, water, and sunlight. You could use the story of the "Three Sisters" (corn, beans, and squash) as a captivating way to illustrate how different plants support each other, much like friends do.

This narrative teaches them about companion planting, instilling cooperation and mutual care values.

Creating a dedicated space for children in your garden encourages ownership and pride in their efforts. If space is limited, this could be a small plot where they can decide what to plant or even a container garden. Equip them with child-sized gardening tools to make the experience more accessible and enjoyable. As they watch their plants grow, they engage more deeply, understanding the lifecycle of plants and the importance of caring for living things.

It's also an excellent opportunity to introduce them to the wonders of nature, such as the role of bees in pollination or how worms help enrich the soil, turning everyday gardening moments into exciting science lessons.

Family garden projects can be both ambitious and rewarding. Consider building a raised garden bed together, selecting companion plants as a family. For instance, you might plant strawberries and let the children plant companion flowers like borage, which helps deter pests naturally and improves the fruit's flavour. As you work together to build and plant, discuss why each plant is essential, focusing on how the flowers attract pollinators necessary for the strawberries to fruit. This project beautifies your space, yields tasty rewards, and strengthens family bonds through shared goals and achievements.

Companion planting offers endless teachable moments. For example, explain legumes' nitrogen-fixing ability and their role in helping neighbouring plants thrive. Such discussions can lead to broader conversations about sustainability and environmental stewardship. Encourage children to ask questions and observe the garden, fostering a sense of curiosity and wonder. These discussions can deepen their understanding of ecology and the importance of biodiversity, laying the groundwork for a lifelong appreciation of the natural world.

Turning companion planting into a cherished family tradition can create lasting memories and instil deep-seated values. Start simple traditions like an annual planting day where everyone helps prepare the garden for spring. Celebrate the season's first harvest with a special meal from your garden's produce, where each family member can pick and prepare their favourite vegetable or herb. Such traditions make gardening an eagerly anticipated event each year and weave it into the fabric of family life, creating a legacy of gardening knowledge and environmental respect that can be passed down through generations.

By integrating these practices into your family routine, you cultivate more than just plants; you nurture a sense of responsibility, cooperation, and connection to nature among all family members. The garden becomes a place of learning and laughter, where every plant—and every moment—has something to teach us about living harmoniously with nature.

8.4 The Environmental Impact of Companion Planting

When you step into a garden designed with companion planting principles, you're not just entering a space filled with plants; you're stepping into a mini-ecosystem where each plant plays a pivotal role in sustaining a healthier environment. This gardening method goes beyond mere aesthetics—it embodies a commitment to sustainable practices that benefit your garden and the broader environment. By understanding the direct impact of companion planting on sustainability, soil health, water conservation, and wildlife habitats, you can appreciate your garden's profound influence on the ecological balance of your local area.

Sustainability

Companion planting inherently promotes sustainability by reducing the need for chemical interventions. Chemical fertilizers and pesticides, while sometimes effective, can disrupt local ecosystems and pollute water sources. In contrast, companion planting uses natural relationships between plants to enhance growth and deter pests. For example, marigolds release a natural compound that repels nematodes and other soil pests, which can protect neighbouring plants like tomatoes. This natural protection reduces the need for chemical pesticides, which not only preserves the health of the soil but also ensures that local waterways remain uncontaminated. Furthermore, by increasing biodiversity in the garden, companion planting helps create a more resilient growing environment. Diverse plantings can recover more quickly from adverse conditions like harsh weather or pest invasions, reducing the need for resource-intensive interventions.

Soil Health

The health of the soil is fundamental to the garden's health, and companion planting plays a crucial role in maintaining and improving this vital resource. By strategically pairing plants with complementary nutrient needs, gardeners can naturally preserve the nutrient balance in the soil. For instance, planting nitrogen-fixing legumes near nitrogen-loving leafy greens can naturally replenish nitrogen levels in the soil, reducing the need for synthetic fertilizers. Moreover, companion planting encourages using plants with different root depths, which helps prevent soil compaction and promotes better water infiltration. The varied root structures also help aerate the soil, which enhances root health and allows microorganisms essential to soil fertility to thrive. These practices contribute to a rich, loamy soil that supports robust plant growth and reduces erosion, further contributing to the sustainability of the garden ecosystem.

Water Conservation

Water is a precious resource, and its conservation is critical in gardening. Companion planting can play a significant role in reducing water usage in your garden. Certain plant combinations can significantly lower evaporation rates by creating shade and reducing surface wind, allowing the soil to retain moisture for extended periods. For example, planting taller crops like corn or sunflowers to shade lower-growing, moisture-loving plants such as lettuce can reduce the need for frequent watering. Additionally, using ground-cover plants like creeping thyme or clover can help keep the soil moist by providing a living mulch that cools the soil and reduces water loss. These strategies conserve water and make the garden more resilient to drought, reducing your garden's environmental footprint and helping you manage water use more efficiently.

Wildlife Habitats

One of the most delightful aspects of companion planting is its ability to attract and support a variety of wildlife. A garden rich in diverse plantings provides habitats for numerous beneficial insects, birds, and small mammals. For example, flowering plants such as sunflowers and lavender can attract pollinators like bees and butterflies, crucial for pollinating many crops and wild plants. Similarly, including dense shrubs or small trees can offer nesting sites for birds, which help control insect populations naturally. These wildlife-friendly practices enhance local biodiversity, improving the local ecosystem's health. By providing food, shelter, and breeding sites, your garden becomes a small wildlife sanctuary, supporting species diversity and promoting ecological balance.

Incorporating companion planting into your gardening practices is more than just a strategy for plant health—it's a commitment to nurturing an environment that respects and supports the natural world. Through thoughtful plant choices and strategic garden planning, you can create a space that not only produces abundant harvests but also plays a crucial role in sustaining the environmental health of your community.

8.5 Companion Planting and Wildlife Conservation

The tapestry of life in your garden extends beyond the plants to butterflies' fluttering wings and bees' soft buzzing. When you design your garden with companion planting principles, you're not just thinking about which plants grow well together but also creating a haven for beneficial wildlife. By choosing a diverse array of plants, you enhance the beauty and yield of your garden and invite an assortment of wildlife that plays crucial roles in the ecosystem.

Companion planting acts as a natural invitation for beneficial insects and birds. For instance, when you plant sunflowers, you're not just aiming for their stunning blooms and seeds. These towering flowers attract bees and birds, which are vital for pollination and keeping pest populations in check. Similarly, herbs such as lavender and fennel are not only great for your culinary creations. Still, they are also excellent at drawing in honeybees and butterflies. Their aromatic flowers provide nectar, which is crucial for the survival of these pollinators, especially in urban areas where natural sources are limited.

Moreover, incorporating plants like yarrow and goldenrod can bolster the presence of ladybugs and lacewings, which help manage aphids and other pests naturally. This method of attracting beneficial wildlife reduces your need for chemical interventions. It supports the local biodiversity, making your garden a part of the solution in urban wildlife conservation.

The potential of companion planting extends to the conservation of endangered species, both plant and animal. By incorporating native plants in your companion planting strategy, you contribute to preserving local flora and fauna. Native plants are more likely to support a broader range of local wildlife, including some species that are rare or endangered. For example, planting milkweed is essential for the survival of monarch butterflies, as it is the only plant on which they lay their eggs and their caterpillars feed. By choosing to grow native plants alongside your usual garden favourites, you help maintain your area's natural heritage and provide a refuge for species that might otherwise face habitat loss.

Creating wildlife corridors in urban and suburban settings is another transformative aspect of companion planting. These corridors enable wildlife to travel safely between habitats, crucial for maintaining genetic diversity and ecosystem health. You can contribute to these corridors by designing your garden with connectivity in mind. This might mean coordinating with neighbours to create a continuous strip of wildlife-friendly planting or ensuring that your garden has various plants that flower at different times, providing year-round resources for wildlife. Such efforts make urban areas more wildlife-friendly, mitigating some impacts of urban sprawl and habitat fragmentation.

Several case studies highlight the positive impact of companion planting on local wildlife populations and ecosystems. For instance, a community garden project in an urban area transformed a barren plot into a vibrant garden with various companion planted herbs, flowers, and vegetables. Over time, the garden provided food and enjoyment for the community. It became a sanctuary for urban wildlife, including bees, butterflies, and birds, previously scarce in the area. Another example is a large-scale restoration project that used companion planting techniques to rehabilitate a degraded wetland area. By carefully selecting plants that supported each other and attracted specific wildlife, the project successfully increased biodiversity in the area, bringing back species that had not been seen there in years. These examples underscore the potential of thoughtful companion planting to restore and enhance local and larger ecosystems, significantly contributing to wildlife conservation.

As you continue to explore and implement companion planting in your garden, remember that each plant choice can contribute to a larger purpose. Your garden is more than just a space for growing food or flowers; it is a potential lifeline for the wildlife in your area, playing a critical role in ecological conservation efforts. By supporting biodiversity through your gardening practices, you help ensure that your local environment remains vibrant and healthy for future generations.

8.6 Continuing Your Companion Planting Journey

As you cultivate your garden, remember that companion planting isn't just about achieving immediate results—it's about embracing an ongoing cycle of learning and experience. Think of your garden as a living laboratory where each season brings new opportunities to deepen your understanding of how plants interact with each other and their environment. This continuous learning enriches your gardening experience, making each year more rewarding than the last.

Approach your garden with curiosity and a willingness to try new things. This year, you pair celery with leeks to determine if you can deter pests. Alternatively, you may experiment with aromatic herbs like lavender to attract more pollinators to your vegetable beds. Whether it succeeds or needs adjustment, each experiment adds to your knowledge base. Sharing these experiences can be incredibly valuable, too. Join garden clubs or online forums to exchange ideas with fellow gardeners. This communal sharing of knowledge helps refine your techniques and introduces you to new concepts you might not have considered before.

Keeping a garden journal or starting a blog about your companion planting adventures can be a rewarding way to track your progress. Document everything from your initial planting plans to the end-of-season results. Include notes on what plant combinations worked well and which didn't, and take photos to visualize your garden's evolution through the seasons. This record serves as a personal reminder of your journey and can also be a fantastic resource for fellow gardeners.

Over time, your journal or blog becomes a comprehensive guide filled with personalized insights that can help inform future garden layouts and plant choices.

Staying informed about the latest developments in companion planting is crucial. The gardening world constantly evolves, with new research, techniques, and plant varieties continually emerging. Subscribe to gardening magazines, follow horticulture experts on social media, and attend workshops or lectures whenever possible. Many universities and botanical gardens offer courses that can deepen your understanding of ecological relationships in the garden. These resources keep you connected to the broader gardening community and inspire your projects. They can introduce you to advanced concepts like soil microbiology or the latest eco-friendly pest control techniques, expanding your horizons and improving your gardening practices.

As you move forward, remember that every plant in your garden offers the chance to learn something new. Whether tweaking a plant combination to improve yield or experimenting with a new variety of heirloom tomatoes, each choice is a step toward becoming a more skilled and knowledgeable gardener. This approach enhances your garden and contributes to the community's collective knowledge, promoting a more sustainable and vibrant world.

In this way, the garden you cultivate produces more than food or flowers—it becomes a testament to your growth as a gardener and a steward of the earth. As we wrap up this chapter, take a moment to reflect on the journey you've embarked on. From the initial planning stages to the daily care and observation, each step has been part of a larger narrative about growth, learning, and connection. Looking ahead, the lessons learned here pave the way for future explorations in gardening and beyond, promising more discoveries and delights as each season unfolds. As this chapter closes, prepare to carry forward the seeds of knowledge you've gathered, planting them in the fertile soil of continued education and shared experience. In the next chapter, we'll explore how these principles apply in your garden and the broader landscape of community and environmental health, underscoring the profound impact your gardening journey can have on the world around you.

Make a Difference

Imagine stepping into a garden where every plant plays a part in a vibrant ecosystem. That's the magic of companion planting, and now you can help spread this wisdom.

Would you lend a hand to someone eager to start their own garden, even if you never met them?

This person is like you—curious and ready to learn, but unsure where to start. Our mission is to make companion planting accessible to everyone, transforming gardens into thriving, sustainable spaces.

Most people judge a book by its cover (and reviews). So, here's a request on behalf of a budding gardener:

Please help them by leaving this book a review.

Your review costs nothing and takes less than a minute but could inspire and guide someone on their gardening journey. Your words could help…

Use the QR code.

Thank you.

Conclusion

As we draw the curtains on our journey through the vibrant world of companion planting, let's take a moment to reflect on the transformative power this practice holds. By integrating companion planting into your garden, you're planting seeds and cultivating a sustainable, eco-friendly environment. This approach fosters biodiversity and champions natural pest control. It minimizes the chemical need, turning your garden into a thriving ecosystem.

Throughout this book, we've explored the science that underpins companion planting, the undeniable benefits of strategic plant pairings, and a slew of practical techniques—from garden planning and pest management to maximizing yields. These key takeaways are your tools, designed to empower anyone, including you, to start and nurture a companion-planted garden, irrespective of your gardening experience or available space.

Remember, transitioning from beginner to confident gardener is a journey filled with learning. Each plant that thrives and doesn't add to your experience. Celebrate every little success and take every setback as a stepping stone to better your understanding and skills.

I encourage you to keep your curiosity and your hands in the soil. Experiment with different plant combinations, adapt to your garden's changing conditions and tweak your strategies as you grow. Share your stories and discoveries within the gardening community, whether online or locally, and let's build networks of knowledge and support that blossom just like our gardens.

By choosing companion planting, you're not just gardening but taking a stand for environmental stewardship. You're part of a more significant movement towards a more sustainable world, where biodiversity thrives, and chemical use in our gardens diminishes.

I am eager to hear about your companion planting adventures! Share your successes, challenges, and lessons learned. Your stories have the power to inspire and educate others in the community, creating a ripple effect of knowledge and passion for companion planting.

Thank you for joining me on this green journey. I hope the pages of this book have sown seeds of inspiration that will flourish in your gardens and beyond. Here's to growing together towards a future where our gardens are not just spaces of beauty and sustenance but also pillars of ecological health and community wellbeing.

Keep planting, keep learning, and may your gardens always thrive in the companionship of plants and people alike. Here's to the blossoming of healthier gardens, stronger communities, and a resilient ecosystem, all nurtured by the gentle yet powerful hands of companion planting.

References

The Three Sisters of Indigenous American Agriculture. Retrieved from https://www.nal.usda.gov/collections/stories/three-sisters

Plant Communication from Biosemiotic Perspective - PMC. Retrieved from https://www.ncbi.nlm.nih.gov/pmc/articles/PMC2634023/

Case Studies: Successful Pest Management on Organic Farms. Retrieved from https://vrikshafarms.com/blog/post/case-studies-successful-pest-management-on-organic-farms

USDA Plant Hardiness Zone Map. Retrieved from https://planthardiness.ars.usda.gov/home

The Scientifically-Backed Benefits of Companion Planting. Retrieved from https://gardenerspath.com/how-to/organic/benefits-companion-planting/

How to Design the Perfect Vegetable Garden Layout. Retrieved from https://plantperfect.com/how-to-design-the-perfect-vegetable-garden-layout/

Container Garden Companion Planting Guide. Retrieved from https://www.permacultureapartment.com/post/container-garden-companion-planting

A Complete, Step-by-Step Rotation Planning Guide. Retrieved from https://www.sare.org/publications/crop-rotation-on-organic-farms/a-crop-rotation-planning-procedure/a-complete-step-by-step-rotation-planning-guide/

The Best Companion Plants for Tomatoes, Plus Tips to Make ... Retrieved from https://www.marthastewart.com/companion-plants-for-tomatoes-8605567

Improving Biological Nitrogen Fixation to Improve Soil Nutrient ... Retrieved from https://edis.ifas.ufl.edu/publication/SS714

Companion Planting for Pest Control. Retrieved from https://journeywithjill.net/gardening/2019/02/26/companion-planting-pest-control/

The New Companion Planting: Adding Diversity to the Garden. Retrieved from https://www.udel.edu/academics/colleges/canr/cooperative-extension/fact-sheets/adding-diversity-garden/

Why should I get my soil tested? - AgriLife Today. Retrieved from https://agrilifetoday.tamu.edu/2023/06/12/why-should-i-get-my-soil-tested/

Best Organic Pest Control: What Works, What Doesn't. Retrieved from https://www.motherearthnews.com/organic-gardening/organic-pest-control-zm0z11zsto/

References

Vegetable Gardening for Beginners: The Complete Guide. Retrieved from https://www.almanac.com/vegetable-gardening-for-beginners

The 12 Permaculture Design Principles. Retrieved from https://permacultureprinciples.com/permaculture-principles/

5 Good Reasons to Adopt the Biointensive Farming Method. Retrieved from https://themarketgardener.com/farming-techniques/5-good-reasons-to-adopt-the-biointensive-farming-method/#:~

Companion Planting: The Ultimate Guide for Pest Control and ... Retrieved from https://ezfloinjection.com/article/companion-planting-the-ultimate-guide/

Crop Rotation for Home Vegetable Gardeners. Retrieved from https://journeywithjill.net/gardening/2019/10/28/crop-rotation-for-home-vegetable-gardeners/

20 Best Hosta Companion Plants. Retrieved from https://www.provenwinners.com/learn/hosta/companion-plants

Companion Planting | Extension | West Virginia University. Retrieved from https://extension.wvu.edu/lawn-gardening-pests/gardening/garden-management/companion-planting

Plant Flowers to Encourage Beneficial Insects. Retrieved from https://hort.extension.wisc.edu/articles/plant-flowers-to-encourage-beneficial-insects/

Ten tips for vegetable gardening during a drought - UC ANR. Retrieved from https://ucanr.edu/sites/ucmgplacer/files/189174.pdf

Why You Should Practice Intensive Planting in Your ... Retrieved from https://www.gardenary.com/blog/why-you-should-practice-intensive-planting-in-your-organic-kitchen-garden

Pollinator-Friendly Native Plant Lists. Retrieved from https://xerces.org/pollinator-conservation/pollinator-friendly-plant-lists

Companion Planting for Pest Control. Retrieved from https://journeywithjill.net/gardening/2019/02/26/companion-planting-pest-control/

Companion Planting With Herbs - Gardenia.net. Retrieved from https://www.gardenia.net/guide/companion-planting-with-herbs#:~

The Future of Gardening: Green Technologies & Sustainable ... Retrieved from https://verdenook.com/articles/future-of-sustainable-gardening-green-technologies-innovations

Companion Planting is key to food security. Retrieved from https://www.renature.co/articles/companion-planting-is-key-to-food-security/

Community gardens and their effects on diet, health ... Retrieved from https://bmcpublichealth.biomedcentral.com/articles/10.1186/s12889-022-13591-1

The Science of Companion Planting in the Garden. Retrieved from https://www.montana.edu/extension/broadwater/blog-article.html?id=1878

Made in the USA
Columbia, SC
05 April 2025